SPARKS

IDEAS TO IGNITE YOUR BUSINESS GROWTH

SHWETA JHAJHARIA

WINNER OF 2 INTERNATIONAL STEVIE AWARDS

SPARKS

First published in 2017 by

Panoma Press Ltd
48 St Vincent Drive, St Albans, Herts, AL1 5SJ, UK
info@panomapress.com
www.panomapress.com

Book layout by Neil Coe.

Printed on acid-free paper from managed forests.

ISBN 978-1-784521-07-3

The right of Shweta Jhajharia to be identified as the author of this work has been asserted in accordance with sections 77 and 78 of the Copyright, Designs and Patents Act 1988.

A CIP catalogue record for this book is available from the British Library.

This book is available online and in bookstores.

Printed in Great Britain

Testimonials

"I am a firm believer that the more you learn, the more you earn. And what better way to learn than from one of the top business coaches in the world.

"Shweta's intelligence, depth of knowledge and experience and dedication to the craft of business building shine forth in this brilliant book for anyone running a business. It is full of great takeaways – irrespective of how long you've been running a business and in several places even eye-opening. A must-read for any business owner who wants to grow!"

Brad Sugars, Founder and Chairman, ActionCOACH Author of *The Business Coach and Buying Customers*

"This book gives you a step-by-step blueprint to start, build, manage or turn around any business. It can make you rich!"

Brian Tracy, author of *Million Dollar Habits*

"Shweta Jhajharia is a dynamic coach who has transformed many businesses and individuals for the better. SPARKS is filled with common sense, accessible advice that will put you on the same path to success."

Marshall Goldsmith, executive coach, business educator and NYT bestselling author, ranked the number one leadership thinker in the world by Thinkers50

"As a connector of people and ideas, I read a lot of books on business and personal success and I can confidently say that very few of them can deliver the structure and clarity that Shweta does in SPARKS."

Dr. Ivan Misner, NYT bestselling author and Founder of BNI

"If ever a book for business owners and entrepreneurs had a great title, SPARKS is it!

"I've had the enormous pleasure of seeing Shweta live — she's an extraordinary presenter in so many ways, not least because she brings the magic of structure into everything she does. And now, at last, she's brought structure upon structure into this great book.

"It won't just give you the sparks that we all need in these amazing times, it'll make sure those sparks ignite a significantly better business than the one you're running right now or indeed, the one you're intending to build.

"Grab it, go with it, flow with it. Like me, you'll love it. And you'll love where it takes you too."

Paul Dunn, Co-Founder and Chairman, Buy1GIVE1

"Working with Shweta has enabled me to grow my business and really sit back and take a bigger, wider view of the business. I started the journey as a manager, with coaching I quickly moved on to be a leader and am now an entrepreneur and investor – something I could not have imagined at the start and my goals are much higher than before.

"Reading SPARKS is like talking to Shweta. You get clear, practical and actionable ideas and walk away with clear next steps!"

Karen Howes, CEO, Taylor Howes Designs

"Maintaining a focus on the key aspects of running and growing a large business is an imperative, that in my experience is all too easily diluted by a multitude of competing priorities. With Shweta's help, I've regained a focus on the business fundamentals and set clear priorities that are result oriented. Clearer accountability is leading to consistent delivery of results and bottom line performance. I recommend Shweta and this book to help achieve those outcomes."

Neil Cooper, Chief Executive, MLM Group

"Shweta Jhajharia distills the essentials of what it takes to run a business into six core areas and then goes on to help the reader gain real insight into each in a very accessible way. This is a book you will want to read and re-read as you face the constant challenges of running a business."

Laura Frost, Director, Aspect Commercial Flooring

"Shweta homes in on the profit potential of a business like an Exocet Missile. In her inimitable, no nonsense way, she quickly helped us identify what we needed to do less of, what we needed to do more of, and what we needed to do better. I wish we'd found her 10 years ago."

Craig Dessoy, Founder and MD, Hugo Oliver

"SPARKS, Ideas to Ignite Your Business Growth taught me stuff I never knew before, but thought I did. That is the magic of working with Shweta – she guides you down the path to realising the full potential of your business."

Mike Keeler, MD, Garnett Keeler

"We have been in running our business for 26 years and worked with Shweta for the past 18 months. She has proved to us that you can never stop learning and improving however long you have been in business. She really is a true inspiration, an incredible motivator, and has an accurate and deep understanding of what it takes to grow a business."

Andrew & Richard Bacon, Directors, Fiesta Crafts

"Shweta is a truly inspirational coach who has transformed how we live our business. The magic in what Shweta does is to challenge you to think differently about the things you think you know, to think in a structured, focused way and to break down your big thoughts into a series of actions that help those thoughts to materialise into new realities. Through its structure in small chapters or 'lessons', this book will be an invaluable resource in helping me to stay on track in my business."

Jan Shury, Joint MD, IFF Research

"Shweta came so highly recommended we couldn't really believe the reality would live up to the legend.

"In less than 3 months we were already seeing a transformation not only in the business but in ourselves as business owners.

"We are enjoying the challenges and without a doubt one of the best investments we have made."

Jane Wagner, Director, WaltonWagner

"If you want a blueprint for success, SPARKS is essential reading. In this comprehensive book, Shweta shares wisdom and inspiration while giving very practical steps in her customary inimitable no–nonsense manner.

"I have benefitted tremendously from Shweta's business coaching which is very genuine and based on walking the walk. "

Ajani Bandele, Founder and Managing Consultant, NetworkIQ

"Shweta Jhajharia has been my business coach throughout a phenomenal period of rapid business development, awakening my ambition and drive to reach further than ever before. Never have I met anyone with such focused determination for others to win, succeed and achieve their dreams. With Shweta, you are guaranteed to receive her very best and my advice to anyone working with Shweta for the first time is to dream big as you are soon to realise your own very best."

Paul Hastings, MD, Reflections Print Finishers

"I was reluctant to even fill out the initial questionnaire sent by Shweta's office, having never had a coach before. However, more than 12 months on, despite questioning at the start whether Shweta would genuinely be able to add value to our very technical and niche business, Shweta continues to amaze me at every session. Her ability to grasp any challenge faced by our business and find a workable (and often exciting!) solution is remarkable. She genuinely is a partner to our business and helps us to maintain our market–leading position in the UK."

Abhishek Sachdev, CEO, Vedanta Hedging

"After 35 years in business, the one lesson I would pass on to anyone is to surround yourself with the best people and learn from them at every opportunity. This book offers a great chance to learn from one of the best mentors anywhere in the world today."

Stephen Reynolds, Owner, Evergreen Christmas Trees

"This is more than just a book – it is the voice in your head, the person that sits on your shoulder guiding you to greatness. Shweta has a remarkable way of delivering insights through artful storytelling, practical examples and proven techniques. A must have book for any business owner who wants to grow!"

Amanda Hamilton, Founder & CEO, Drink me Chai

"This book encapsulates many of the real world business techniques that Shweta has taught me over the last 2½ years, as my coach. Delivered in her straight–talking style, these tools have grown my business and the fun of running it, while reducing the stress. She has made the seemingly complicated, straightforward."

Miles Brown, Owner, Brownings Garage

"Since working with Shweta and her team not only has my business doubled in turnover, my confidence and clarity in what is achievable has also doubled. I have learned what I expected to learn, but more than that is to learn the unexpected."

Vicki Young, Owner and Designer, Nalla Designs

"Having been in business for over 20 years, I thought I knew it all. And then I realised that the more you know, the less you do. We came to a point when we recognised that all these great things that we know we should be doing, were simply not being done. We reached out and accepted the fact that a coach could help and that has made all the difference. We now set goals, monitor them and achieve them. The difference to our business has been significant.

"I believe that the biggest gift I can give my best friends and best clients is to introduce them to Shweta. This has in fact been the case on more than one occasion.

"If you really want to increase the size of your business and do well, read this book and implement the ideas in it. Or even better, ask a business coach like Shweta to help!"

Yahya Mirjan, Director, Granite and Marble International

"It's life changing. As a business owner you must have the correct mindset. Shweta has helped us realise that we can dream big and we can achieve it. She comes alongside you and step-by-step shows you how to get there. You need to actually step out there and do something different to achieve something different."

Teryl & Leslie Abrahams, Directors, Bodies Under Construction

"When I was first approached by Shweta I could never have imagined the impact she would have on my business and personal life.

"Having run a reasonably successful business for many years I was at a point of not knowing how to take my business to the next level. My staff lacked the enthusiasm and drive that I still had but with Shweta's help, we managed to identify the issues that were holding my business back and put in measurable systems to take the business to the next level.

"Shweta without a doubt has been one of the best business investments I have made."

Graham Hill, Managing Director, JJ Roofing Supplies

"Shweta is the most incredible coach with amazing energy, focus and purpose which she uses to challenge, support and drive business leaders to improvement and success.

"I have been working with Shweta for two years and it has had a profoundly positive effect on me and Future Platforms, the business I run.

"With SPARKS, you can now tap into a lot of the ideas she has taught me and many small business owners. As you read through the anecdotes and stories, I'm sure you'll identify yourself and the challenges you face in a few of them – the way I did myself. If you want to grow your business and improve your own performance I recommend you buy this book and learn from the UK's best business coach."

Adam Croxen, Managing Director, Future Platforms

Disclaimer

Contents

Acknowledgements

I am truly grateful to have had the opportunity to learn from hundreds of world-class thought leaders – directly through interactions with them and indirectly though articles, books, videos and audios.

As I read through the final drafts of this book, I realised that this was really a book of my heroes. Every story, every idea, every theme has contributions from someone I respect: people who know me – my teachers, friends, clients, team and family – and people who I know, through knowledge that they have shared. I have tried to acknowledge them throughout the book with quotes and inspirational ideas from them.

I do hope that I have been able to translate some of my learning and made it accessible to a few more people.

I wish for you to be your own hero and continue to be inspired by others and by yourself.

The Beginning

"Please stop."

"I don't want to waste my time any further. Let's meet after a couple of years when you know what you're talking about."

Graham got up and walked out of the room.

I sat stunned, speechless and shocked. This was the fifth business prospect who had walked out on me.

Have you ever been in a situation where you knew that you could help the other person but every time you tried you felt that you were hitting a wall of resistance?

That is exactly how I felt in the winter of 2008 as I dreamt of building my newly founded business. Sitting in my office with tears in my eyes, the world and my dreams seemed to be getting hazier with each passing day. A whirlwind of questions was going through my head.

Was this the right decision for me? How long will I be able to sustain this?

"Shweta, this is not Unilever where having the title Global Marketing Manager will make a difference. This is a small business with hard realities which you know nothing about."

Graham's words were still echoing in my mind. "Do you even realise how many businesses are struggling and expecting to go under in this financial recession?"

"Forget about my industry. You have been in this country less than a year – you understand nothing about the people, the economy and the way business is done here."

"Please stop. I don't want to waste my time any further. Let's meet after a couple of years when you know what you're talking about."

I sat staring at the computer screen blankly as it broke to the screen saver.

Suddenly, I heard a knock on the door and my husband, Amol, walked in. Amol is my rock. When I get upset, he stays calm. When I am worried, he reassures me. When I am confused, he helps me get clarity.

"What happened, Shweta?"

And, of course, that was just the trigger I needed. I began to break down.

"Amol, I don't know how I can get my belief across. I don't know how I can inspire confidence in people especially when I am so new to the country. I just can't get these voices out of my head. I must have been crazy to leave my fast track corporate career to try and run my own business – against my parents' advice. How can I possibly let them down? My sabbatical period is running out and I still have nothing to show for the last few months. I just don't know what to do."

Amol listened quietly as I poured myself out and then said, "First, take a deep breath Shweta."

I took a deep breath as I tried to calm the tremors I was now feeling.

"Are you confident that you can make a real difference to Graham's business?"

"Of course!"

It took me a split second to answer that question.

I knew that with my Masters in Business Administration and successful career with Unilever working across sales, brands, marketing and multiple strategic business units, I had a good grasp of the fundamentals of a business. I also knew that I had invested in one of the best business coaching franchises in the world – ActionCOACH – and had access to decades of experience across businesses, countries and coaches.

"Graham doesn't know that. How can you make it a no-brainer for him?"

Have you ever had a moment where you just had a blinding flash of 'obvious'? When something has been right under your nose and you've been consistently ignoring it? That was the moment for me.

I spent a restless evening and night as the initial thoughts of a solution began to crystallise in my mind.

Next morning at 9am, I called Graham.

"Hi Graham. This is Shweta. I've thought quite deeply about our discussion yesterday and would like to meet you again. Can we meet in the next two hours?"

"Shweta, I said two years not two hours."

"Graham, I don't think either of us has two years to wait."

I'm still not sure what he heard in my voice that day, but he agreed to meet. "OK, fine. Let's meet up. But we'll have to keep it short."

Just as we were 24 hours ago, we sat face to face again. This time Graham's 6ft 2inch broad-built English demeanour was unfazed. He was clearly in no mood to waste time.

I laid out a blueprint of his potential business opportunity. As I reiterated how we could together grow his multimillion pound business even further, I sensed once again his growing scepticism.

I said, "Look Graham, whatever I tell you will sound like a fluff because every Tom, Dick and Harry out there may claim that they can make your business better. I totally understand that. But let me tell you one thing. I'm happy to stick my neck out on this one."

Graham smiled. "Did you read my mind there?"

"Graham, I have put myself in your shoes. I understand how you're feeling."

"So, here's the deal: in the first six months of our working together, if you do everything we agree on and the business's incremental gross profit is not more than what you have invested, I will refund the difference, no questions asked."

It was Graham's turn to sit in stunned silence. I waited for what felt like ages.

And then he said the magic words, "Let's do it."

And an exciting journey began for both of us.

I would love to say that the next few months were simple and easy and everything was fairytale like. Far from it. Every step we took was often excruciatingly difficult – from the very first step.

"Let's get started. Could you share with me your numbers for the last three years, current year's projections, marketing planner with budgets, your key team members, key measurables and…"

"Hold it Shweta. I can give you my last three year's accounts but I don't have any of the other stuff you are asking for."

I felt humbled by the honesty of this successful multimillion pound business owner who wanted to grow even further and engage his team in the process of growth. Simultaneously, I felt nervous at the magnitude of the task ahead of me.

It was an experience that taught me the power of swapping your 'wanting to win' mindset with a 'refusing to lose' mindset. There could not be any excuse I would rely on anymore – recession, being new to the country, being younger and less experienced than the client, having no experience of the industry – none of these could be allowed to become a reason for failure.

Step by step, Graham and I approached the business and the mindsets in the business and worked together for a lot more than the initial promise of six months. The chart opposite shows the growth trajectory of the business.

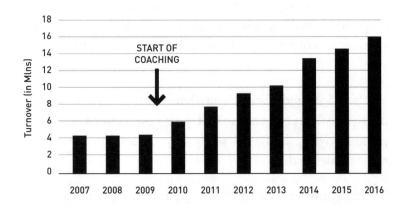

With year on year double digit growth, Graham and his team have continued to pick up multiple awards over the last several years: Best Community Impact, Best Financials, Entrepreneur of the Year, Best Retail Business, to name just a few.

And, in the process of working with hundreds of business owners over the last few years and implementing a multitude of strategies to make them even better, my business has picked up dozens of awards too – a testament to all the hard work my clients, my team and I have invested in the quest for growth.

As my father taught me, "Happiness is neither this nor that. It is simply growth."

I love that what I do gives me an opportunity to work with amazing people and make both their business and personal lives happier. It has given me an opportunity, just like now, to engage and share with you.

I might not know you personally, but I am certain that, like most business owners, you recognise that while you may be doing well, you could be doing even better.

Possibly, you are trying multiple things in your business – across marketing, sales, hiring talent – but these are not really working out. There is only a trickle of enquiries and customers into your business.

It could be that you are working long hours every day and missing out on all those moments with your loved ones and asking yourself the question at the end of each week, month or year: Where did the time go?

It might be that you are worrying more about paying your staff than paying yourself. And maybe your business is frustrating you, costing you money, time, effort and progress – so much so that you are beginning to question if this is what having a business really means.

Now, just imagine…

Your business is growing at a predictable double-digit rate every year, with a great sales pipeline. You are attracting good clients and your marketing machine is working not by chance but by design.

Your team is absolutely aligned with the business and where you want it to be. They are always right behind you and beside you and you all are moving in the same direction. You enjoy working with your team and not constantly wondering: Ugh, do I really need to deal with that? You look forward to engaging with them and together your business is making a difference in the marketplace and in the world.

You are doing exciting things – things that you love to do with people you love. You are feeling confident and you are thinking beyond the defined paradigms. You are planning on expanding to different locations, acquiring other businesses and contributing to the community. In the truest sense, you can feel the gratitude and bliss of owning your business and of having the ability to add value to people's lives.

Would you agree that to move from where you are to where you want to be you need to DO something different and BE someone different?

My purpose is to help you build an even more successful business and this book is a guide to the elements that will help you on that journey.

Before we start, let's define what we mean by a successful business.

In my view, a successful business is a profitable entity that can work without you.

The purpose of any business is to provide solutions – answers to problems that the potential customer has. When it adds value, it gets value in return i.e. profit. If the business is profitable, it has the first crucial component of success.

If your business is profitable but stalls every time you take a holiday, you don't really have a successful business; you have created a bad job for yourself (and perhaps a few other people). The litmus test is the question: Would my business continue to perform if I were to take three months off? If your business can run without you, it has the second crucial component of success.

Your business is an asset and you truly only own an asset when it generates a positive return on your investment and has a saleable value. If you are critical to the business, the business has very little saleable value without you. This is indeed possible to achieve for most businesses but requires persistence and commitment and work in areas that do not directly positively impact the current profitability of the business.

Multiple studies have found that most businesses never make it past the £1 million turnover mark in their lifetime. For those that do, a significant majority again never reach and exceed the £10 million turnover mark. Think about why that would be the case.

Where is your business right now? And where would you want your business to be? And what are you willing to do for that? With the odds stacked so significantly against you, how likely do you think it is that your business will be among the small minority of businesses to cross the £1m or the £10m mark?

The fact remains that your time in your business is limited and running out. Newer, better, faster and younger businesses are being born as you read this and they will challenge everything you know about your industry and your business. Watching the speed at which my son understands and works with technology is just staggering to me. As a mother I feel proud, but as a business owner I am concerned. Not only does this generation require us to tap into them as talent, the future business owners from this generation are going to make staying in the game for current businesses extremely difficult. Moving with a sense of urgency has become a critical competence for all growth-minded business owners.

Your business is an amazing vehicle for you to experience different things, push boundaries, reach out to the community and make a difference. Perhaps now may be the right time for you to redefine your destination, the speed at which you want to move to that destination and the rules you want for the journey.

The Framework

Working with multiple businesses across different sectors, I have realised that there are six key elements which a successful business needs to have. It is the inadequacy of one of these elements which often sabotages the potential growth of the business.

I've put these together in a framework because I believe that frameworks are extremely helpful in bringing clarity to situations. While one framework may not be the perfect answer to every problem in the business, they often give you the ability to make faster decisions which can often mean the difference between success and failure.

Most of the situations I've seen business owners struggle with can be categorised into one of the cells of the 6M Model.

Mindset

Everything in life and in business is created twice: first in the mind of the business owner and the team and then in reality.

Too many businesses spend an inordinate amount of time see-sawing between success and failure. Every time they do well, they begin to do things that become the seeds of their downfall and then when that happens, they tighten their belts and start all over again. These business owners often fail to reflect on their own limiting mindset which stays with them as they take the roller coaster ride of business profitability.

Unfortunately, whatever strategies and tactics you know and whatever systems and talent you are working with are only sustainable if you are also consistently working on your own and your team's mindset.

Often when I ask a business owner what they do, they respond, "Oh, I'm just a small business owner."

I cringe at that description. Why would you choose to be a small business owner when you could be a big business owner in training? For 'just a small business' everything is small: their approach, their mindset, their strategies, the way they think of their team, their overall skill, and crucially, their profitability. As a big business owner in training, your approach, your mindset, your results are all big. You unlock the ability to think massive action, massive change and massive results. You take on more risks and are prepared to fail because your dreams and your goals are worth the risk.

The fact remains that your business will always reflect you. Remember the neck of the bottle is at the top. Working on improving your mindset is the first step to overcoming the bottlenecks in your business.

And there are tested and proven habits of success which can help you ensure that you are consistently in a state of peak performance.

Mastery

Having the right mindset is important but not sufficient.

Often business owners 'fall' into their business. They get into the business by accident or due to circumstances – a good idea or a turn of events. They learn how to do the technical work required to be good at offering the product or service their business is offering and begin to tell themselves, 'I can figure it out' when running a business.

How long does a professional take to become a professional? Think of a plumber, an electrician, a solicitor, an accountant or any other professional. How much work do they have to do and how much do they have to learn before you would employ them?

How long would you want a dentist to have studied and worked before you are comfortable sitting in front of him/her with your mouth open for treatment?

How confident would you be of wiring your own house if all the training you had was a one-day workshop showing you how to do it? Would you call yourself a professional?

Now think about how many years of experience one needs to become a professional business owner.

Unfortunately, only in the profession of business can someone call themselves an entrepreneur or business owner in under four minutes – the time it takes to register a business or change your online profile.

The barriers to entry into the profession of business are extremely low. Is it therefore any surprise that the failure rate is so high?

This is where Mastery comes in. How do you make sure that your decisions in business are better than what a coin-flipper would make?

Given that most business owners spend most of their waking lives in their business, how well have you mastered this profession? How much time and money have you really invested in learning this profession?

Before you can build your business empire, you need to build the foundation of the business and master the key elements of your business.

Mission

With a great mindset and complete mastery of business, but without clarity, you may just be all dressed up with nowhere to go.

A journey of a thousand miles begins first by knowing where we are going.

The one thing that I've consistently seen successful businesses have is a clear idea of where they are going and a plan on how to get there. Despite this reasonably well-known fact, most businesses do not think of trying to put together even a one-page document that helps them and their team see where the business is heading.

Imagine setting off every day from your home not knowing where you are going and just picking a random route hoping it will get you somewhere interesting.

Most business owners feel that given that business is so volatile, planning just does not make sense as things can change all the time. Imagine hearing that from the pilot on your next flight, "Folks, the weather is quite unpredictable today and all our systems are out. So, we're just going to keep flying until we see someplace that looks good to land and you will then have arrived." Perhaps the journey would be fun, but not many people would sign up to it again and again. Why do people then insist on doing exactly that with their business? And then wonder why their team is not feeling enthused and aligned with what they are trying to do.

A lack of clarity in business has untold costs: massive amounts of time, effort, energy and talent expended in the wrong direction.

Ask yourself the question: If I walk into my business and ask each of my team members where we are heading, will I get the same answer? If your answer is not a resounding Yes! you may have work to do in defining the mission of the business.

Money

The true litmus test of a strong mindset, mastery and mission is in the money that the business makes.

Your business speaks in the language of numbers and in the language of money. This includes the accounts that most business owners only really do for the government and it includes the assets and liabilities you have in your business, your profitability, your margins, your revenue and growth and the numbers that lead up to your business generating revenue.

One of the most crucial elements of money for most businesses is having a constant stream of prospects and customers to ensure growing revenue and cash flow.

Building a sales and marketing machine is an important step to building a business that can generate consistent profitability and growth.

Marketing as a concept and in scope has evolved significantly in the last decade. Unfortunately, most business owners do not understand how to go about marketing and are often overwhelmed with it, leading them to either do nothing or go down every rabbit hole that different marketing gurus point them towards.

And when things don't work, they begin to lose heart and conclude that marketing just does not work for their business. They keep losing money and tinkering with different aspects of their funnel in the hope that something will work.

Money is perhaps the one sphere in which a significant amount of wasted effort in businesses can be averted – by learning the fundamentals and applying them systematically.

Management

The first four elements bring the desired growth of the business and carry within them the growing pains of a business.

What's the difference between starting and growing a business and managing a growing business? What skills and competencies does a great manager need and how are these different from what an entrepreneur needs?

Building a robust sales and marketing machine gives your business growth. What helps a business maintain and leverage on that growth is management.

The first step is to find the right talent. Unfortunately, a significant number of business owners still hire the old-fashioned way – the FDBD methodology or, less formally, the Friend's Daughter's Babysitter's Dog-walker approach! They feel that when they know someone in any capacity and rely on them to do one thing, that would automatically translate to them being reliable and competent in another capacity.

Also, most business owners are lazy recruiters – they choose convenience over the correct approach and tell themselves they do not really have the time to hire right. Unfortunately, they soon find out that hiring another person has increased their workload because now they do two people's work and manage another person!

I've found that business owners are overwhelmed by their constant need to manage people and a very simple switch in thinking can make a big difference to their management ability.

You never manage people. Most businesses have adults working for them – mature, grown-up individuals who can think for themselves and take care of themselves. The moment you accept this, you can start focusing on what really makes all the difference – managing the activities of people.

Managing the activities of people is where we can start applying objectivity and metrics – starting from clarifying what the activities are that people in the team need to be working on, what the measurables are that will tell us that the activity has been done poorly or well, and the indicators of performance on these activities.

The next level of your business and its true potential may be beyond what you could ever achieve by yourself. The key to unlocking this potential is two-fold: learn how to find the right people and then learn how to manage their activities.

Methodology

A profitable business built with the right mindset, mastery, mission, sales and marketing machine and management skills may still be unable to work without the business owner if the crucial element of methodology is missing.

A lever is something that helps reduce the amount of input required to achieve a certain amount of output – or increase the output for the same amount of input.

So how would you like to achieve 'More with Less' in your business? That is what a good methodology helps you achieve – business leverage.

Most business owners still work the way they worked when they were a team of one. They deal with everyone and everything in their business in a unique and non-repeatable way.

Here's a mantra you need to take to heart to master leverage: Systemise the routine and humanise the exception!

There is, unfortunately, a limit to what any individual can achieve alone – and this limit applies to you too. Unless you learn to leverage your people, your systems and your structures, you will continue to struggle against a ceiling in your business – something that is unfortunate, especially if you have the willingness to work hard, lots of passion and ambition and the drive to make things bigger and better.

You need robust methodology and systems in every part of your business to help unlock its potential and make your business even bigger and better.

Our Approach

"Life is too short for a long story."

Mary Wortley Montagu

Mindset, Mastery, Mission, Money, Management and Methodology are all important in building a profitable entity that can work without you. As you build each of these capabilities in your business, you unleash more and more of your own and your business's potential.

Your business is often a reflection of you. And your habits and mindset are what define you. The first step in moving to the next level in your business may be improving your mindset and resolving any embedded issues that may be holding you back. When working with business owners, we help them implement The Proven Success H.A.B.I.T.S.™

These six proven and fundamental mindset principles help business owners stay in peak form to ensure they can lead from the front while aligning their team's behaviour to the needs of the business.

Next, mastering the game of business by continually improving your skills and competencies, you need to invest in learning more before you can earn more. To have mastery of their business, we help businesses implement The Firm Foundation Formula™ to build the simple yet strong foundations of their business and help them understand the financials and critical numbers driving their business. If nothing else, it prepares them to ask their team and advisors meaningful questions and guide them towards business growth.

Often business owners do not understand the language of business and are not able to dig deeper into areas they have no expertise in – eventually giving up and taking 'GUT' decisions. While as a woman I understand the importance of gut and intuition, as a business owner I recognise that if business decisions are based solely on GUT then it is simply an indication that the business owner Gave Up Thinking for that decision. The Firm Foundation Formula™ helps business owners significantly increase their probability of success.

Your business mission is the guiding light that leads you and your team towards greater success. As a business coaching firm, we make sure that business owners working with us build clarity for themselves and their team. The Default Action Planner™ translates this mission to goals, goals to a plan, and a plan to the actions required to achieve the goals. The Default Action Planner™ is a 13-week action plan, with clear timelines and accountabilities for each action point clearly defined, which systematically helps businesses define their destination and then map out the step by step journey that will take them to the destination. The Default Action Planner™ enables the business owner to have a more automated way of working on a weekly basis rather than allowing the fires of a typical work day to jeopardise their strategic action points.

Once the Mindset, Mastery and Mission are in place, ensuring your business can generate a constant and consistent flow of money is crucial before you can even call it a proper business. This is where we work with businesses to build The Ultimate Sales & Marketing M.A.X.I.M.I.S.E.R.™ – the chassis on which every business is built and grown. We identify and profile the target person for the business and base decisions on marketing channels, strategies and execution plans on this. The objective of The Ultimate Sales & Marketing

M.A.X.I.M.I.S.E.R.™ is to build a machine that can create measurable, predictable and consistent results and make marketing precise rather than prolific.

Once you have established a consistent flow of money in the business, the game of business begins to transform to one of management more than entrepreneurship. This is where the importance of building and managing a team comes in. One of the consistent issues I've seen businesses face when trying to grow is the problem of finding the right talent; they often spend an incredible amount of time doing it wrong. To handle overwhelm and time involved in recruitment we have built a powerful process that significantly increases the chances of you finding the right talent while at the same time reducing the amount of time spent on finding talent – The Productive S.O.U.R.C.E. Code™.

Recruitment is, of course, only the first step – now you must ensure that the team integrates and succeeds. This is the challenge of retaining talent and incentivising the team and providing them with the right training. This is where The Top Talent Toolkit™ comes into play where we break down which activities the business owner needs to manage and how an incentive system should be put in place to keep the team motivated and aligned with the business goals.

Finally, the crucial piece of the puzzle – making the business work without you. This is where the power of systems and leverage comes in and we define The SYSTEM Levers™ to bring all the different threads of the business together to enable the business to work without the business owner. There are four crucial parts of the organisational structure that need to be systemised before you can take your foot off the pedal and this is what we cover in The SYSTEM Levers™.

While Mindset, Mastery, Mission, Money, Management and Methodology are all independently extensive topics, this book has been written to be readable, without an overload of information. The purpose of the book is to provide sparks of ideas to reignite the fire you already have inside you. Where there is a story to be told which demonstrates the point, I've chosen to include it.

I have used models and frameworks to make concepts more palatable and focused on content and anecdotes of how different businesses have addressed the various issues they faced.

 I have also highlighted several resources (highlighted as the symbol left) available to help you apply the ideas you will learn in this book.

I have used a core framework – the 6M Model – which helps pull all the pieces together; however, feel free to dip in and out of the various pieces. Most of the content has made a tangible difference to several of the businesses I work with – not only knowing the content but implementing it practically.

My commitment to you is that all the ideas in this book have worked for businesses. They may need to be adapted to make them work for you but these sparks have the potential of transforming your business, if you let them.

Part I: Mindset

"Watch your thoughts, they become words;
watch your words, they become actions;
watch your actions, they become habits;
watch your habits, they become character;
watch your character, for it becomes your destiny."

Lao Tzu

The Opposite of Fear

The opposite of fear is not courage – it's faith.

Most people spend an inordinate amount of time fighting or succumbing to the realities of the present. They battle every day against the immeasurable amount of negativity outside and inside themselves. Unfortunately, they often do this without ever directly facing the realities that these fears and negative talk exist.

Successful people realise that they are ultimately responsible for creating a positive and driven environment for themselves – an environment where they are creating positive energy and affirmations for their own inner self.

Here's a short tale that emphasises how each one of us is responsible for our own attitude to life.

One evening an old Cherokee told his grandson about a battle that goes on inside people. He said, "My son, the battle is between two wolves who live inside us all.

"One is evil and represents anger, envy, jealousy, sorrow, regret, greed, arrogance, self-pity, guilt, resentment, inferiority, negativity and ego.

"The other is good and represents joy, peace, love, hope, serenity, humility, kindness, benevolence, empathy, generosity, truth, compassion and happiness."

The grandson thought about it for a minute and then asked his grandfather, "Which wolf wins?"

The old Cherokee simply replied, "The one you feed."

Success and positive attitude are a choice and not a given. Each one of us can create the environment in which they will be successful, which means that each one of us is responsible for our own results.

So, the key question becomes: How do we create and maintain the environment for our own success in our minds such that it becomes a reality?

Here's a simple exercise that has been used by some of the most successful people in the world:

Step 1: Define your ideal reality

Define how you would want your life to be in the future: What are the things you would like to have? How would your relationships be? What would you be doing? What kind of human being would you be?

Make a long list of this ideal reality and boil it down to the ones most important to you.

Step 2: Visualise your ideal reality – every day

Spend time every day visualising that your ideal has become the reality. For some people, writing down works better in helping them imbibe this reality. The important thing is to allow your emotions to be involved in visualising this reality. You need to remind your emotive and hence your subconscious self how much you want this reality.

Step 3: Affirm your 'being' – every day

The next step is to create the images and words for success and positive results in our mind. An exercise which I recommend for affirmations is to create your list of 'I AM' statements based on your ideal reality and repeat these to yourself at least once every day.

There is enough scientific evidence now to corroborate the positive consequences of encouragement and the negative consequences of derision. We are unfortunately in a world where people do not hesitate to correct and put down other people. Even more unfortunately, we do this to ourselves all the time too. An exercise of positive affirmations helps negate some of these influences and builds our own ability to accept that we can be part of the ideal reality.

You can curate your thoughts every day to take control of your destiny. Can you start today?

Step 4: Act towards your ideal reality

This is often the step that most people who believe that the universe conspires to work for you forget. You still need to do the work.

There was once a devout man who did not know how to swim. As chance would have it, he fell overboard on a trip abroad a cruise ship – luckily wearing a life jacket. He avidly started praying for help. A couple of hours later, a small fishing boat came up to him and the fisherman offered to help. The man replied, "I am fine, my God will save me!" Puzzled, the fisherman paddled away.

This happened again twice and the man's response was the same, "I am fine, my God will save me!"

After hours of paddling in the icy cold water, he died. Being a devout, of course, he went straight up to heaven.

His first question to God was, "I have been a devout all my life and always believed in you. Why then did you not help me when I was dying and praying for help?"

God replied, "Well, I did send three boats!"

The Blue Pill

"When everything seems to be going against you, remember
that the airplane takes off against the wind, not with it."

Henry Ford

One of my clients, a successful business owner, once started talking about some of the goals he had for himself and his business when he first started and how they compared to his goals today. As we discussed how his thinking had evolved in the 10 years he had been in business, we realised that as he had achieved one measure of success, time had also taught him to compromise on his bigger goals and ambitions. He felt comfortable where he was in his business and was loathe to over extend himself or his business to drive further growth.

How many of us reach that plateau in life and in business? We convince ourselves that what we have is good enough and there really is no point in trying to relive our dreams. Those dreams were of a forgotten youth when we didn't understand how the world worked. The passion, energy and drive that first got us started in business and saw us claim success after success seem to be a thing of the past and long forgotten.

What happens when you face the truth about what your business could really achieve if you started rebuilding it with the same passion, energy and drive that you first had? Only this time you also add to it the years of experience and best practice you have accumulated and the strategies that have worked for thousands of other businesses across the world.

In the film *The Matrix*, Neo (Keanu Reeves), the hero of the film, is introduced to a mysterious man named Morpheus. Morpheus talks about the Matrix and the truth that Neo is just a small part of the Matrix and one of the Matrix's 'slaves'. Morpheus then presents Neo with two pills – a blue pill and a red pill – and explains a choice to Neo:

"This is your last chance. After this, there is no turning back.

"You take the blue pill – the story ends, you wake up in your bed and believe whatever you want to believe.

"You take the red pill – you stay in Wonderland, and I show you how deep the rabbit hole goes. Remember, all I'm offering is the truth – nothing more."

The question for the business owner/entrepreneur is whether reality or truth is worth pursuing. Taking *The Matrix* film into context, the blue pill will leave us as we are, in a life consisting of habits, of things we believe we know. We become so comfortable with our status quo, and build imaginary walls of stability around ourselves, that we do not seek truth or the right way.

The red pill, on the other hand, symbolises passion and drive along with risk and questioning the status quo. It forces us to ask 'What if?' and 'Why?'

Asking these questions ultimately leads us to a choice: Do you continue to ask and investigate, or do you stop and never ask again?

Are you willing to take the path of discovery and change – and implement radical changes in your business to make it resilient, competitive, and forward looking?

Are you willing to move on from the illusion of what is perceived as safe and challenge the same principles which worked for you in the past? Do you want another chance to explore the limits of what you and your business can achieve?

As business owners, we are presented with these pills again and again. Neo chose the red pill. Which one would you choose?

Master or Slave

"We think of effortless performance as desirable,
but it's really a terrible way to learn."

Daniel Coyle

There is a verse which resonates with me and which I use
to remind my clients of how important it is to consistently
monitor one's thoughts, words, and actions.

I am your constant companion.

I am your greatest helper or heaviest burden.

I will push you onward or drag you down to failure.

I am completely at your command.

*Half the things you do might just as well be turned over to me,
and I will be able to do them quickly and correctly.*

I am easily managed; you must merely be firm with me.

*Show me exactly how you want something done, and after a few
lessons I will do it automatically.*

*I am the servant of all great people and, alas, of all failures, as
well.*

*Those who are great, I have made great. Those who are failures,
I have made failures.*

I am not a machine, though I work with all the precision of a machine plus the intelligence of a person. You may run me for profit or run me for ruin; it makes no difference to me.

Take me, train me, be firm with me, and I will place the world at your feet. Be easy with me and I will destroy you.

Who am I?

I am habit!

Are you the master of your habits or a slave to them?

Which is the one habit you have which is stopping you from being a lot happier and even more successful? What are you going to do today to start breaking away from this habit?

The Price We Pay

"The price of discipline is always less than the pain of regret."

Nido R Qubein

In life, we either pay the price of discipline or the price of regret.

While we pay these prices in all areas of our life, for most business owners the results are most apparent in their daily, monthly and yearly business results.

The price of discipline might be that daily dose of exercise, that moderation in life affairs, eating habits and relationship strategies (such as open and honest communication) or in business: the weekly team meetings, building and maintaining default diaries, testing and measuring marketing strategies and developing systems. The absence of these daily little disciplines accumulates, day by day and year by year until you and your business inherit the long-term consequences of these misdeeds.

Most of us have had personal experiences where the lack of daily discipline comes back to haunt us. Arrogance, ignorance, or a combination of both offers very little help and life and the business world really don't care if you claim either or both as your excuse. We'll each pay for it, one way or another, sooner or later. Remember, daily discipline weighs mere ounces in the 'load of life' while lifelong regrets can feel as if they weigh tons...

...the sweat of discipline and sacrifice is nothing compared to the pain and regret of inaction.

Here are some ways to clarify for yourself which of these you're paying the price for:

- Pay attention to your quiet, yet persistent, inner voice that urges you to change.

- Listen to the people around you: family, friends, team members etc. Are they trying to tell you something?

- Look at areas of your life for which you feel, or have felt, regret of some kind. Are you repeating old behaviours even today?

- Tune into life – its issues, demands, expectations, as well as all the signals and messages you're receiving. Are you hearing or ignoring them?

Ask yourself:

- What can you learn from this?

- What might you change? And what should you leave the same?

- What price will you have to pay to achieve, get or experience it?

- Will it be worth the cost?

- **What do you need to do** to break the pattern of behaviour that leads to regret?

- **Who do you need to be** to establish the discipline needed in every area of your life and business?

Change Your Swing

"It is 9:58 and it is now. Tomorrow at 3:00 it will be now. On my deathbed, it will still be now. Since it will always be now, learning to respond to now is the only thing there is to learn."

Hugh Prather

In 1996, a 20-year-old Tiger Woods was named the Sports Illustrated Sportsman of the Year and the PGA Tour Rookie of the Year. In 1997, he won his first Masters with a massive 12-stroke victory at Augusta, becoming the tournament's youngest ever winner.

Then he changed his swing!

He called in Harmon, his coach, and told him that his swing was too reliant on timing. "Anybody can time their swing for a week, but I want to do this for a career," he said. Tiger wanted to build a system which would work under the extreme pressures of a world championship. "When the pressure's on, good mechanics will overcome nervousness. At the same time, the guy who has good mechanics will get less nervous because he knows the other guys will break down first."

Throughout 1998, Tiger Woods struggled and won only once. Still he stood by the new swing he was learning and practising.

At the Byron Nelson in 1999, Woods famously signalled what was to come with a phone call to Harmon from the range. "I got it," he said.

Between 2000 and 2002, Woods won 19 times on the PGA Tour, with six majors, including a stretch where he won four majors in a row – the so-called 'Tiger Slam'. Golfers today often talk about Woods' Harmon swing as one of the greatest swings in the history of the game.

There are several ideas in the above story that apply to businesses. Here are some that stand out.

Critically Examine Your Success

Ask yourself what really has made your business successful. Often, business owners tend to look for reasons for whenever they fail and spend an incredible amount of time identifying the things that the business should not be doing. When things work, however, they peg it down to their superb sales/entrepreneurship/creative skills. You need to constantly ask yourself what the actual reasons for your success are and how easy they are to replicate.

Accept Change

No business is immune to change. For a business's long-term survival, it is important to take a step back and re-evaluate how you deliver your core product/service and message. You can either reach acceptance through the cycle – Denial, Anger, Bargaining, Depression, Acceptance – or simply start there.

Accountancy as a profession changed relatively little until the introduction of computers. Now as cloud-based finance systems revolutionise the market, the profession is throwing up massive opportunities for those willing to embrace change.

Plan for Change

The first step is to recognise the need for constant change. Every year, if not every quarter, set aside at least a few hours to analyse your business and the potential and likelihood for change. One of the oldest and most established tools for doing this is a SWOT (Strengths, Weaknesses, Opportunities and Threats) analysis.

Look at what your customers and competitors are saying and doing. Ask your suppliers for input. You'll be surprised how much competitive information they usually have. Go online to research what people are saying about products and services like yours. When was the last time you googled for 'I need a [your product]'?

Create a specific plan of action to implement the change. Remember that people rarely like the idea of change, so there will always be a lot of pressure to keep things as they are and hope for the best.

Stick to the Plan

Often in every process of change, there is a dip before the steep climb begins – in profits and in motivation levels. Remember that failure and success are not at two ends of a scale; they are at the same end of the scale – failure is right before success.

The successful businesses are those that exhibit 'grit' in the pursuit of their goals.

Play for the Long Term

Pick the top things that you believe have worked for your business since inception, or for the last 20 years. Then list three reasons that threaten each of these things not working in the next three years. Build your business with the end in mind – robust systems and a good team should be running the business when you are ready to retire/move on. If you are most of the strength that keeps your business alive, you need to rethink your business swing!

Seek Best Practice

Often, business owners are so ingrained in their day-to-day that they can't see the wood for the trees. When was the last time you were humble enough to ask for help – from a colleague, partner, supplier, coach or mentor? Who do you know who could help you take a step away and look at your business from the outside-in to identify areas and strategies where you can start the process of small and massive improvements?

Change your swing, then do it again!

Boiling Frogs

"The truth is that the first changes are so slow they pass almost unnoticed, and you go on seeing yourself as you always were, from the inside, but others observe you from the outside."

Gabriel García Márquez

If you place a frog in a pot of boiling water it will understandably scramble out quickly.

However, if you place it in a pot of water at room temperature and don't scare it too much, it will stay put. If you then set the pot on a stove and gradually turn up the temperature, something very interesting happens. As the temperature gradually increases, the frog will do nothing. In fact, it will show every sign of enjoying itself. As the temperature continues to increase, it will start becoming groggier until it no longer has the strength to climb out of the pot. Though there is nothing physically restraining it, it will sit there and boil.

The frog's psychological apparatus for sensing threats is geared to sudden changes in its environment, not to slow gradual changes. In psychology, this phenomenon is called sensory adaptation. The frog's ability to adapt to the slowly increasing temperature is not a good thing for it in the long run. But is this not how a lot of change creeps up to us in life? Change is in fact often slow and gradual rather than sudden.

In helping businesses deal with change, I have discovered this phenomenon repeated – we get accustomed to terrible situations and don't realise how hot the water is getting. If we were to describe our current situation to a 10 years younger self, our younger self would probably be shocked beyond belief.

Why do we stay in water that is approaching the boiling point? Is it because it is a lot more difficult to look inside and self-evaluate? Quite often it takes someone from the outside to see the gradual change building up and awaken the slumbering entrepreneur.

Sometimes, however, we fear that any attempt to jump out of the water will land us straight into the fire. We are paralysed by the prospect of change. So, instead of jumping, we tread water hoping that the heat will soon stop. Is it risky to try to change the environment or jump out of the pot? Or is it riskier to continue to adapt to the increasingly unpleasant environment?

We will not avoid the fate of the boiled frog until we learn to slow down and see the gradual processes that often pose the greatest threats. We need to constantly question how comfortable we are and whether the situation is good for us and our business.

What kills the frog is not the boiling water but its own inability to decide when it had to jump out.

We all need to adjust with people and situations, but we need to rethink when to adjust and when to change the situation. There are times when we need to face the situation and take the appropriate action.

We must decide when to jump. Deciding not to jump is also a choice. Blaming the water for changing around you is pointless.

Why You Are Like an Iceberg

"Keep away from people who try to belittle your ambitions.
Small people always do that, but the really great ones make
you feel that you too can become great."

Mark Twain

What really sank the Titanic? The image that most people conjure up in their mind of a mountain of ice bobbing above the water is not really what sank the ship. That was only 10% of the iceberg; what really sank the great ship was the 90% that is not visible and below the surface of water. How does this relate to you as a business owner?

Let's use the iceberg as a metaphor for you, as a business owner and as a leader of a business, and your identity.

You should understand that what is visible, above the water, is just 10% of what determines your decisions as a business owner. This bit above the surface is your behaviours – how you conduct yourself in business, the parts that are visible to your team.

The concept of the Identity Iceberg is useful in clarifying the idea that what you show to the world – the 'doing' that you do – is only really 10% of who you are. The 'being' part of yourself – the skills, beliefs, values and identity – is mostly invisible to those around you and often even to yourself.

And it is that 90% where you will find your strength and your confidence.

Not only that but the environment in which you place yourself – the water in which you, as an iceberg, sit – dramatically matters in your personal and professional development.

Continuing the metaphor of the iceberg, your environment can be warm and drain from your being, or the water can be a cold expanse from which you draw strength and continue to grow.

But unlike the iceberg metaphor, how the environment affects you is a choice that you can make. You can boost yourself and learn to absorb positivity from your environment, or you can allow the negative comments from those confidence vultures eke away at your strength and confidence. You may not be able to control the environment itself, but as the adage goes, you can control how you react to it.

In the end, it doesn't matter how good you are now, or that your identity is a bit weak now. Icebergs grow and so can you. What's important is that you grow and become better by taking simple steps that pave the way for reaching the heights of business success.

Developing the right mindset for the business through positive self-talk and ignoring all the negative thoughts of the confidence vultures that surround you is indeed important.

But that won't be enough to achieve your business goals.

You should take the initiative and develop the right skills, belief, value, identity and environment, which are the hidden parts of the Identity Iceberg for a business.

Your Business Skills

Do you really know what the skills are that you excel at? Where do you need work? What are the business skills that differentiate your business from others? If you don't know, then you should really put your mind to it.

Identifying and improving your core business skills is an important part of an Identity Iceberg that you should not ignore at any cost. The fact is the things you are skilled at you end up doing more of.

If you're good at cooking, you will cook more.

If you're good with numbers, you'll do more number crunching and finance work.

If you're good at interacting with people, you'll do more client-facing work.

If you want to become a better business director, you need to understand your business in a holistic sense.

You need to consciously develop the skills that you're NOT good at because you DO have to deal with all areas of your business. This is critical because your skill level will determine your actions and behaviour. If you don't have the skills, you won't do it – and your business will suffer.

Your Business Beliefs

The next level deeper is your belief system.

When we are kids, our teachers and our parents will often tell us, "You're good at English." Or maybe it's Maths, or Science, or Art. Whatever the subject, they encourage you with the best intentions.

However, what this does is set an anchor in your mind that formulates a belief and develops into an opinion: Oh yes, I'm very good at English. But it can also be flipped and become a negative anchor: I'm not very good at numbers.

Maybe those belief systems have worked for you, or maybe they have impeded you. Either way, they've created core beliefs that have fundamentally affected who you are.

What you need to do as a business owner is to create the right sort of anchors for you to develop your business in the best way possible. You cannot go into business saying, "I don't like numbers" because numbers are a critical part of every aspect of your business.

Equally, you can rarely go into business saying, "I don't like people" because most businesses are designed to solve people's problems – and if you cannot interact with people well, you will find it difficult to sell your solution to them. Not only that, but you will also have difficulty understanding how to work with your team.

Your Business Value System

This isn't the same thing as beliefs – this is taking it one step deeper. Beliefs are more to do with what you think you are and aren't capable of. Your values are what you consider as right and wrong, correct and incorrect.

Often people have a lot of 'head trash' caught up in their value systems which stops them from achieving what they really want to achieve.

The best example of this is how people view the idea of money and making a profit.

Take a step back for a second and consider how you see money. Many people see money as 'evil' – which means you're not meant to talk about money and making money is not good. That's fine; if that is your value system then go for it and seek out the goals that you really want to seek out.

However, almost every business owner I know DOES want to make money but is filled with this sense that it's not a good thing to focus on or think about.

Well here's my viewpoint on money: if your business is not making good money – not 'enough' money, but GOOD money – what that says is you are not adding enough value to enough people.

Once you reach out to a bigger market, in a systemised and scalable way, you will automatically be bringing in more money – and that's a good indicator of the value you provide.

There is a core relationship between the value you provide and the money you get in return. So, you should ask yourself what are the core values that you hold and, most importantly, how they affect the way you run your business.

Your Business Identity

This is the final depth of the Identity Iceberg. Who are you at the core? What do you put after 'I am…'?

What are you? What defines you? Are you a mother? Are you a business owner? Are you good at numbers? What is it that really makes you who you are?

Drilling down through these different levels of the identity is an important exercise for any business owner. Knowingly or unknowingly, almost everyone carries around a lot of anchors with them that may be affecting their judgment in business.

Focusing on your business belief, values and identity will add value and help you create the foundation on which your business can grow. However, there is one final thing to consider when it comes to your identity: your business environment.

Your Business Environment

An iceberg cannot survive in a tropical ocean – it must be in a very cold expanse of water. Equally, even the most entrepreneurial spirit cannot grow into a successful business owner if they are not surrounding themselves with an environment that nurtures their identity.

What books are you reading? Who do you have around you advising you on your business decisions? What webinars are you attending? Are you taking notes at workshops and reviewing those notes later?

This is the environment that you create for yourself – and you should be creating one where you are forcing yourself to become better.

As you develop the right beliefs, values and identity within yourself and nurture the right environment around yourself, you will significantly enhance your ability to move your business towards greater success.

I Am the Greatest

"I don't count my sit-ups. I only start counting when it starts hurting. When I feel pain, that's when I start counting, because that's when it really counts."

Muhammad Ali

I once got a sharp response from one of the recipients of an email I had sent out inviting people to one of our events. They said I sounded 'conceited' and that the email was 'totally off-putting'.

So, I went back to re-read the email and try to understand where this person was coming from, and I began to understand. And then I also understood why I had not naturally changed the tone of the message when I had first written it.

On re-reading the email, I could see where this person's sharp response may have come from. There was a line I had written where I was talking about why I was offering tickets to the event for free that said '…because you may not yet have met me and therefore have no idea how good I am'.

I do accept that that sounds quite conceited and could perhaps have been worded better. However, I also thought of one of Muhammad Ali's greatest quotes:

"I Am the Greatest; I said that even before I knew I was."

I believe that this quote is important for business owners to understand, because what he is talking about is a confidence mindset, which is one of the key ingredients of success in business, and not just sports.

The former boxing champion is talking about the idea that you must have the strength and belief in yourself to push yourself to the top if you really want to get there, no matter what others around you say.

No one else – not even your best friend – is going to tell the world that you are the greatest. You are the one who must do that for yourself, you must motivate yourself, and you must lift yourself up if you want to continue to achieve great things.

Confidence Vultures

One of my business coaching clients recently had won an award and emailed his contacts about it. Someone replied to him with a tirade of why he was not good enough to have won that award.

Obviously, my client felt wounded by the remark and was shaken in confidence in his product and business.

I explained to my client that there are some people out there that we call 'confidence vultures'. These are people who have learnt that feeding off other people's confidence can be a way to boost their own self-esteem.

As you climb in confidence yourself, you will face these people. There is no doubt that they will come out of the woodwork. You must be able to protect yourself, and that confidence that you have built, from such people.

The quote from Muhammad Ali that I mentioned above indicates how to do just that. You need to have the strength within yourself to say 'I am the greatest' even when others try to tell you otherwise.

You can, and should, build your own confidence. And when you learn how to enter that cycle of building your own confidence, you can then push your confidence as high as you want it, regardless of which vultures swoop around and peck at you.

Remember, You Are Like an Iceberg

It helps, in this context, to review the concept of the Identity Iceberg.

Remember that the environment in which you place yourself – the water in which you, as an iceberg, sit – dramatically matters in your personal and professional development. Your environment can be warm and drain from your being, or the water can be a cold expanse from which you draw strength and continue to grow.

But unlike an iceberg, how the environment affects you is a choice that you *can* make. You can boost yourself and learn to absorb positivity from your environment, or you can allow the negative comments from those confidence vultures eke away at your strength and confidence.

You may not be able to control the environment itself, but you can control how you react to it.

Is it a Cultural Thing?

As someone who was not raised in Britain, I am constantly learning, understanding and adapting to British culture. There are a lot of significant differences between India's and Britain's cultures, I will tell you that!

What I find really intriguing is that the natural exuberance of Americans is often described by the British as 'brash' or 'gung ho'. Yet I must admit, when I have witnessed such brawny positive attitude it is in some of the most successful and driven people I know. Perhaps it is natural for the British to be more reserved and respond more deeply to those around them. But perhaps there is some small learning to be gained from our brothers and sisters across the pond in learning how to boost our own self-esteem as well.

Affirmation Becomes Conviction

In the end, Muhammad Ali constantly talked about self-motivation and about creating your own drive and creating your own success. I think that is why his words so often resonate deeply with me – his mindset is something I fully agree with.

Guard your positive self-belief with passion. Refuse to hang around with people who do not believe in how worthy you are and how much more successful you are going to become.

I truly believe that *It is the repetition of affirmations that leads to belief. And once that belief becomes deep conviction, things begin to happen.*

L before E except after A

> "To go into any enterprise is to know how to get in,
> then you have to think how to get out."

Jim Rohn

They say that the only place where Learn does not come before Earn is in the dictionary. And correct Action is what is required for both learning and developing.

Goals and benchmarks allow you to see some aspects of the future. You don't need to have the exact destination and path, but you do need to know where it is that you want to go. In other words, benchmarks will help you achieve your goals relating to the business.

So, you have developed your business and it is running, now what?

How do you want to progress? Do you want to further add some products or services or do you want to invest in something new now?

Most entrepreneurs get into business for reasons that are not entirely evident to an outsider at first glance. The following three reasons are among the most basic:

1. To make more MONEY and/or have more control over how they make it.

2. To have more TIME for themselves and can choose how to spend it.

3. To get CONTROL over their lives and their own destiny.

However, very few business owners are fully able to realise these goals. What prevents them from achieving their goals? Why haven't they done anything about it? Why have they allowed themselves to accept mediocre results?

According to the Conscious Competence model, learning happens through four distinct stages:

Unconsciously Incompetent – I Don't Know that I Don't Know

Consciously Incompetent – I Know that I Don't Know

Consciously Competent – I Know that I Know

Unconsciously Competent – I Don't Know that I Know

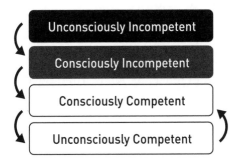

We can use the example of learning to drive a car to exemplify how a person moves through these stages in almost every learning journey.

In the beginning, you do not even know all the things you need to know to be able to drive a car. You have not yet been shown how little you know and how much you must learn.

If you decide to learn driving, you begin to understand the controls on a car and realise that negotiating roads is much harder than you initially thought. Often, you fail to do well and feel some level of hopelessness and frustration on ever being able to learn.

Given time, feedback and regular practice, you move from getting things mostly wrong to starting to get the hang of it. However, you do need to continue to be careful and fully aware while driving. In other words, the competence comes with effort.

With further practice, driving gradually becomes second nature to you and you do it without thinking – or while thinking about something else. You can now apply the rules habitually and unconsciously.

Often, as I speak to business owners, I find that while in the technical aspects of their business they are almost at unconscious competence, as far as running the 'Business of Business' is concerned, they are *Unconsciously Incompetent*.

They *are* unaware of the missed opportunities they have forfeited in the past, and more importantly, the massive results they could achieve NOW and in the future if only they knew what really was achievable and how it could be achieved.

These business owners have an obligation to themselves, their family, their employees and the communities they live in to do the very best that they can. They have a responsibility that is the cornerstone of our society. Yet these same business owners are faced with the reality of simply surviving, paying their bills and hoping that there's enough left over to keep going another day. That isn't right!

As a coach, I share in this obligation. I take very seriously the responsibility to be the very best I can be, not only for my own business but also for my clients and prospective clients. Just as Action is a critical step towards making a business successful, often the first step is recognition of the possibility of your business being somewhere significantly better than where it is today.

Develop a passion for learning and action. Success in life and business will follow.

The Prince of Thieves

"Procrastination is the thief of time – collar him."

Charles Dickens

Perseverance is perhaps one of the most important things you need to be successful. The opposite of perseverance is procrastination. Perseverance means you never quit. Procrastination means you either never get started or never get finished.

Often people who procrastinate reason that they are perfectionists and everything must be just right before they can get down to work. No distractions, not too much noise, no telephone calls interrupting, and of course they must be physically and mentally well too. The other end of procrastination – being unable to finish – also has a perfectionist explanation: 'I'm just never satisfied. I'm my own harshest critic. If all the i's aren't dotted and all the t's aren't crossed, I just can't consider that I'm done. That's just the way I am, and I'll probably never change.'

Do you see what's going on here? A fault is being turned into a virtue. The perfectionist is saying that his standards are just too high for this world. This fault-to-virtue syndrome is a common defence when discussing weaknesses, but has very little to do with what's really behind procrastination.

Usually, the basis of procrastination is fear of failure. That's what perfectionism really is, once you take a hard look at it. What's the difference whether you're afraid of being less than perfect or afraid of anything else? You're still paralysed by fear.

What's the difference whether you never start or never finish? You're still stuck. You're still going nowhere and overwhelmed by whatever task is before you. You're still allowing yourself to be dominated by a negative vision of the future in which you see yourself being criticised, laughed at or losing. This negative vision of the future is really a mechanism that allows you to do nothing. It's a very convenient mental tool.

Remember, in business, perfection is the enemy of good.

Turning procrastination into perseverance involves a few powerful principles that foster productivity and perseverance instead of passivity and procrastination.

1. Break it down
2. Write it down
3. Set a timeline
4. Take action

These techniques, though straightforward, are extremely powerful and effective productivity techniques that allow you to put an end to procrastination and help you get started with achieving your goals.

Speed in Business Isn't Enough

"Strategy without tactics is the slowest route to victory.
Tactics without strategy is the noise before defeat."

Sun Tzu

Every morning in Africa, a gazelle wakes up, it knows it must outrun the fastest lion or it will be killed.

Every morning in Africa, a lion wakes up, it knows it must run faster than the slowest gazelle or it will starve.

It doesn't matter whether you're the lion or the gazelle – when the sun comes up, you'd better be running.

The world is changing at an unprecedented pace. The digital revolution is upon us. Speed is the new currency of business.

There are a surprisingly large number of business owners who are entranced by the 'need for speed' in everything they do. What they often forget, however, is that there is a crucial dimension that makes all the difference in the journey of a business: the difference between speed and velocity.

Speed is generally defined as how fast an object is moving: 20 miles an hour, 120 miles an hour etc. Translating this to your business, if work/decisions/activity is not happening, the speed is zero and where there's a lot of movement happening – a frenzy of activity or fast decision making – there is a high speed.

Velocity, in contrast, is defined as the rate at which the object changes its position. So, for example, imagine you're at point A and you take one step forward, and you take one step backward and come back to the original point A. In this case, your speed could be 40 miles an hour, but your velocity will be zero because the displacement has been zero. Velocity therefore is speed in a direction.

Now when you think about this, there could be lots of frenzied activity, lots of pace, lots of action, a lot of activities getting implemented in your business. But the question that you need to ask as a business owner is: Is it leading to positive displacement? Is it moving me in the direction that I want to move?

Because just having speed in the business is not sufficient, what you need to do is to choose velocity over speed. When you look back at your business a year from now, this choice can make all the difference to where you find your business.

As far as quotes are concerned, I believe business owners should identify more with Wayne Gretzky, who has been recognised by many as the greatest ice hockey player ever. His ability to read the game was unrivalled and when asked how he did it, he simply said, *"I skate to where the puck is going to be, not where it has been."*

The Ultimate Sophistication

"Kiss slowly, laugh insanely, live truly and forgive quickly."

Paulo Coelho

There is a famous study which was done with a class of undergraduates, and they were split into two groups. One group was asked to memorise a two-digit number and the second group was asked to memorise a seven-digit number, and then both groups were asked to go out and take a walk in the hall. When they came back, they were offered a slice of cake and a bowl of fruits as options. Surprisingly, the group which had to memorise the seven-digit number was twice as likely to pick up a slice of cake than the bowl of fruits.

What Makes Willpower So Important?

Why it's important for you to understand this is because in your business, when you must achieve goals, you need willpower. And the part of the brain which is responsible for that willpower, or takes care of that willpower, is located right behind your forehead and that is called the pre-frontal cortex. This part of the brain is responsible for short-term memory to keep you focused, to give you strong willpower, to deal with abstract information and make it more granular.

What happens generally is that when you are setting your goal, if it's not specific enough, if it's abstract or if it's too much or too big, then there is a cognitive overload for this part of the brain. And in that case, willpower suffers.

Abstract vs. Reality

So, going forward, if you are really committed to achieving your business goals or personal goals, the distinction that you need to make is rather than focusing on abstractions you need to focus on some very simple specific behaviours, which help your brain to bring in that willpower to support you to achieve that goal.

So, for example, if you say just at a personal level, 'I need to become healthier' or 'I would like to have a better, fitter body.' Instead of that, if you tell your brain clearly that a simple behaviour that you need to have is to go out for a three-minute walk after dinner, the chances of you being strong and having a stronger willpower is a lot higher compared to being abstract. And that's when your brain comes into the picture and supports you with your goal achievement.

Death of an Entrepreneur

"On the one hand, we all want to be happy. On the other hand,
we all know the things that make us happy. But we don't do those
things. Why? Simple. We are too busy. Too busy doing what?
Too busy trying to be happy."

Hal Elrod

I have often heard it said, 'Once an entrepreneur, always an entrepreneur'. An experience, however, made me pause and think again.

My family and I had booked into a bed and breakfast as part of a short trip around Wales. The B&B was quite well rated despite only having been around for a few years. The place was a beautiful building run by an elderly couple, George and Katie (names changed). Katie welcomed us and helped us settle in. She was the ideal hostess, helping us with dinner options and in deciding what to do around the area.

When we sat down for breakfast the next day, I could see that Katie loved to chat with the residents and we struck up a conversation. We had been very impressed by the décor of the place and could see that a lot of money had been spent in making it look the way it did – probably a little more than required.

As we conversed, Katie told us that they had bought this property around 15 years earlier from the profits of George's booming business. They had lived in it with their large family until around seven years ago, when they had had to close their business and decided to convert their house into a B&B.

I am obviously keenly interested in business success and failure so this piqued my interest and I was keen to delve deeper into what had happened to the old business. At this point, George came in and Katie passed the conversation to him.

George described his old business. He had been on the cutting edge of the digital revolution 30 years ago! He was servicing expensive analogue printers and converting them into digital ones – before most people in the country even had a clue what the fuss was about. He had been one of the most respected technicians in the country with his business pushing the £1m turnover mark every year.

However, as manufacturers gradually stopped producing analogue printers, George's business proposition became unviable and he had to close down the business in 2007.

Unable to let go of this great opportunity to seek business advice for my business coaching clients, I asked George his three top learnings from his life as an entrepreneur and he happily obliged.

1. Commit to your clients

"The one thing that defined the success of our business was our commitment to our clients. Our clients knew that we would never let them down and would always be there to support their machines. This often meant on-the-spot decisions to fly across Europe and fix machines – and stay there until they were fixed, which could take over a week.

"Our clients kept coming back because they knew they could rely on us."

2. Get help

"I remember there was a time when I used to boast smugly that my business was recession proof and it made more than a £1 million every year. The printers we serviced were used in the printing of packaging material of big name cereals and confectionery and these would still be needed when the economy was down. Through the long and hard days of putting one foot in front of the other, I did not even pause to think that getting outside help or experienced business advice could actually make my life easier and my business better.

"One of the things that destroyed my business was a deal I agreed with a customer to become a potential distributor of our cutting-edge product. I signed off distribution exclusivity to them and they did nothing for two years on my product – time in which they were able to build a competing product and get it entrenched into the market!

"I was the best at changing analogue printers to digital. Everything else about my business I learnt along the way – and I realise now that not only did I not do a lot of things that a good business should do, several of the things I did, I did after making expensive mistakes that I could have avoided."

3. Don't forget to live life

"I remember once when I was running at the airport to catch a flight and as I shoved past someone to reach the check-in counter, I got a tap on the shoulder and the person I had just shoved aside said, "You need to slow down, mate! You'll have a heart attack!" I laughed it off then but as I reflect now on the time I missed with my family and the physical constraints I now have to face, I do realise that, while clichéd, there is a lot of value in that single piece of advice – to slow down and enjoy the journey."

George had wistful tears in his eyes as he recounted the last part of his story. "The manufacturers moved to digital printing and our whole line of business was wiped out. We used to have a map of Europe with little lights for all our clients," he said. "I saw the lights go off one after the other over the last three years of my business and there was very little I could do. Firing the people I'd worked with for decades was one of the toughest things I have ever had to do."

"I don't think I have it in me to do it all over again now. This B&B is really Katie's business – I only help her run it."

As we left the B&B, I thought of all the entrepreneurs I work with and recommitted to making sure that they got the best of what they deserved in their lives and in their business.

The Spirit of Business

"Argue for your limitations and, sure enough, they're yours."

Richard Bach

Successful leaders sometimes believe that they do not need to change that much. After all, they are already successful. However, while they have many things going for them, there are often just a few areas in which their behaviour or activities need adjustment – and those few areas impact their overall image in other people's eyes. More importantly, what people often don't realise is that sometimes the very things that have led to their business being successful in the past are now keeping it at a plateau and preventing further growth. The things that brought you 'here' are different from the things that will take you 'there'.

Most people who choose to work with a coach are people who want to do even better. They want their businesses to achieve more and recognise that they may need to change their behaviours to make that happen.

While it is true that some of the changes are required at a deeper level, sometimes at the identity level, the truth is, most of the time, there are behaviours that need to change. What most people do not realise is that while changing behaviour is rarely easy, there has in recent times been a lot of research to lay out ideas and steps that make the process simpler.

As a deeply spiritual person, I am constantly looking for parallels between some of what behavioural psychology is discovering and the ideas and concepts developed by sages in history. One of these is the parallel between the Hindu 'Trimūrti' and the process of behavioural change.

The 'Trimūrti' (/trɪˈmʊərti/) is the trinity of supreme divinity in Hinduism in which the cosmic functions of creation, maintenance and destruction are personified as the three Gods: Brahma the creator, Vishnu the preserver, and Shiva the destroyer/transformer.

The parallel outlines the different and sometimes conflicting behaviours that each of us have and helps us understand the balance required to continue to move forward. There are new behaviours that you need to create and old ones that you need to either preserve or eliminate.

Create: Brahma

This is perhaps the easiest part of the parallel to understand. I firmly believe that the first step to behavioural change is often the creation of new habits – and then using these new habits to replace the older ones.

What behaviours do you have that could be improved? When you think of yourself five years from now, what new behaviours would you want to see in yourself? Most successful business owners are driven to constantly improve and do better and this is an idea they often take to quite eagerly. The irony is that the urge and instinct to create is not something that comes naturally to us. Most human beings find it difficult to accept change, so many of us get comfortable with *doing* more when, really, we need to start being better. When something has been working long enough, we tend to become satisfied and comfortable. There is no real pressure or urgency to achieve more, we begin to reduce the effort required to move to the next level.

Here is where the challenge of creation comes in: create positive change in your behaviour by *choice* not *necessity*. When sales are down, making changes to your business to generate more sales is a change you are making out of necessity.

However, if your sales are steady and your business is surviving quite comfortably, that is when you can look at making changes to generate even more sales, which takes you to a whole new level of success. Creating is about focusing on improving the things that are already doing well.

Of course, this is not limited to just your behaviour in business. The opportunity to make positive changes to your behaviour can be found in every aspect of your life – from improving your health, to changing the way you treat people, to your lifestyle habits. The exercise of behavioural change almost always helps not only with business but also has far-reaching effects into your personal life as well.

Do this exercise now. Take 15 minutes to think and list down: what aspect of your life could you improve right now? Just choose one thing that you want to make better and make it something that you do not need to make better, but want to make better. Choose one thing to improve and, this week, begin the process of creating the change.

Remember, information by itself is not useful. It is the application through action that leads to transformation. Start with just one change.

Preserve: Vishnu

Where creation is the fun and exciting part of the process, preservation is often the part that most Personality 'A' types forget to appreciate. The words 'change' and 'preserve' sound like opposites. The truth, however, remains that most successful people have got there through the compound effect of accumulating and preserving wealth over time.

In the book *The Millionaire Next Door*, Tom Stanley and William Danko pursued the truth of who the millionaires in society are and how they have created their wealth. Their key finding was that the typical millionaire was not the one driving the flashy car and living in an upscale neighbourhood. Quite the contrary, the ones with most wealth had got there through the simple habit of saving and investing and living well within their means – preserving.

What if you could improve your business just 1% every week? Guess how much your business would have improved in one year?

68%!

Now what if you could improve yourself by 68% every year – not through the process of creation but through just marginal improvements and preservation of your good behaviours? Does that not make it a lot more worthwhile?

Small changes do make a massive difference in business and in life. Preservation of what is already going well is a critical component to creating long-term success for yourself and your family. This often does not mean status quo but gradual improvement, which by its very nature does not generate the 'excitement' that creation entails. Often, the very same instinct and passion that gets people excited about creation makes them ignore preservation.

An owner of a restaurant I once spoke to was having difficulty with the new branch she had opened. "Customer feedback is saying that the quality of my signature French toast at the other store is inconsistent." She had opened her new café after the booming success of her first one – success that was driven by her signature style of making French toast. She thought expanding into a new location was the best way to generate quick growth, and had set it all up quite quickly to take advantage of the season.

However, as she set up her new store, while she hired someone talented to cook, she had not directly trained the new person in her unique signature dish. She had not taken the steps to carefully preserve the part of her café that had created her greatest success and, thus, had not succeeded as dramatically as she should have in her new location. The work of systemisation is the work of preservation, and generating processes to replicate what you already do well is necessary before moving on to creating new change elsewhere.

This also applies, perhaps more so, to personal and behavioural change. As you focus on creating new parts of yourself, make sure that you have systemised and reinforced the habits and behaviours that have brought you your success.

When you are considering taking steps to change things and become greater, first look back at what you have already accomplished. Take a close look at your business and write down one thing that you and your employees do well. It may be having a fantastic company culture and how everyone interacts and helps each other. It may be a product that is the absolute best on the market. It may be the way your customer loyalty is earned through inspiring customer service. It may be difficult to pin down just one, but I urge you to choose just one thing.

Write it down on a post-it note and stick it up on the wall near your desk. Remind yourself every day that this is the part of you that needs to be preserved – because it is that one thing that will be worth keeping, no matter what else happens.

Eliminate: Shiva

Embedded in the process of creation is the process of destruction. New habits can only take root if you allow some of your older habits to give way.

We live in a world where activity and 'Just Doing It' is revered and unfortunately laziness is looked down upon in all its forms. I find it surprising the amount of activity I see in businesses and in people that just needs to not exist.

In the words of Peter Drucker, "We spend a lot of time learning what to do. We don't spend enough time learning what to stop."

It is often easy to confuse the process of preserving with tinkering with your business and your behaviour and staying busy maintaining a comfortable, mediocre business – one that is less exciting and has a much smaller impact than you can and want to make.

Have you ever moved house? Or even just rearranged the furniture in your room? If you have, you will understand how tormenting and yet liberating it can feel to throw out old things that are not useful to you anymore. The torment is there: I know I have not used it in three years, but I may need to; I have a strong emotional connection to it even though it is actually stunting my growth; maybe this is the secret to my success. However, when you do finally toss it out, you realise how much clearer your space and your mind is – and notice the areas in which you can improve.

As a successful business owner, you may ask yourself: What should I eliminate? and come up with no answer. Ask your team, your suppliers, your customers, your partner and your children – you'll be surprised at how long the list could be. Choose the activities and behaviours you want to get rid of. And then 'Just Stop It'.

Behavioural change happens through the balance of creation, preservation and elimination – the interactions and presence of Brahma, Vishnu and Shiva. Often when people fail in the process of change and improvement, it is through focusing on one of the above at the expense of the other two. Each has its place in the process of change and a time when each God is the most appropriate to call upon.

Accept: Buddha

"God grant me the serenity to accept the things I cannot change, the courage to change the things I can, and the wisdom to know the difference."

Serenity prayer

How likely is it that there are things in yourself and in the world around you that you cannot change? If, like me, you think that there will always be some aspects that are beyond your control, take solace in understanding and accepting – call upon Buddha.

Most driven and successful business owners do not like to hear the word 'acceptance'. Mainly because they see it as giving up, as defeat by another name, or that it is something that is 'unachievable'. So much so they will drive themselves into the ground fighting their battle in the hope that the war will take care of itself.

The business owners who end up with the most growth personally and in their business are keenly aware of the situations where they are powerless and aware of the elements of their identity that still require more work.

Most business owners, however, do not want to hear that they are ever ineffective – in fact, most people in general do not want to hear it. When we do, we often reject that notion and act out, determined to find *some* way to be effective. The result is that we usually end up doing even more damage through our non-acceptance.

However, often, if we accept the things we cannot change, we can let those parts go and focus our time, energy and brainpower on the parts we can do something about. We begin to focus on things that are within our 'Circle of Influence' and move away from conversations and struggles that take us nowhere.

What is the one thing that you need to accept as being beyond your 'Circle of Influence'?

Part II:
Mastery

"I fear not the man who has practised 10,000 kicks once,
but I fear the man who has practised one kick 10,000 times."

Bruce Lee

Colour By Numbers

"Attempting to succeed without embracing the tools immediately available for your success is no less absurd than trying to row a boat by drawing only your hands through the water or trying to unscrew a screw using nothing more than your fingernail."

Richie Norton

A client once told me the following story, which I thought held a key business insight.

One of my neighbours, from a well-off family, did not have any children and decided to adopt. After a few months waiting for the right match, she was finally told that they had found a match. The child they had matched was of Chinese ethnicity and my friend was delighted to take on the responsibility of this beautiful six-month-old baby boy.

In the months after I'd heard the good news, I started seeing less and less of my friend – something I put down to her being busy with raising the child.

One day, I saw her returning home just as I was returning too and started talking to her. She talked of how much of a delight raising a child was and the different experiences she was having. She also mentioned that she had taken up Mandarin lessons, which were occupying whatever little time she had left.

I was impressed at her sincerity and asked her what made her decide to take the lessons.

Her response was, "Well, you know that the child I've adopted is ethnic Chinese. He doesn't speak yet, but when he does, I want to be able to understand what he is saying."

I found the story hilarious but what also struck me was the fact that most business owners are exactly like that mother, with the business as their baby except that they are not sincere enough to learn the language their business speaks in – the language of numbers.

When your business loves you, it'll tell you, in numbers in the bank. When your business is ill, it'll tell you, in cash flow, growth and profitability numbers. When your business feels that something is going wrong, it'll tell you, again, in numbers. The question is simply will you be able to understand what your business is saying?

Learn the Language of Numbers

Think of these words: season, simmer, whisk, purée, marinate, blanch, dice, fold. The common thread here is that each of these has a very special meaning to a chef. A professional chef will not only understand the words, but also know when and how to apply the technique of doing it just right.

Now think of these words: Profit, Sales, Cash Flow Receivables, Assets, Equity, ROI, Average Value Sale, and Conversion Rate. These are the equivalent words that a professional businessperson not only understands, but also applies whenever they make a decision about their business.

However, note that these are not just words – each of these is in fact a number. If you hope to be successful in business, you must become fluent in this language of numbers and know how to apply them directly.

Also, note how these numbers are not accountant-speak. While you need to understand your financials, the real core of the language of numbers includes non-financial numbers that are critical to every major decision in your business.

Learn the Key Metrics for Your Business

The key metrics of your business are the numbers that are critical to make informed decisions to reduce risk and increase return at every point of the business lifecycle.

Here are some of the key metrics you should observe in different parts of your business to manage risk:

In marketing you should be measuring:

- Conversion rates from various strategies
- Average response rate of campaigns
- Return on marketing investment

In sales you should determine:

- The average pound value of your transactions each month
- The number of transactions each month
- The activity each salesperson undertakes to meet targets

In team management you should be thinking about:

- Your ratio of interview to hire
- Your turnover rate
- How truly 'objective' your team objectives are

- Your return on each employee

As a leader you need to ask yourself:

- How many decisions do you retract on?

- How many of your decisions are based on numbers rather than using your 'gut'?

- When you delegate, do you evaluate the value of your time released versus the potential costs of errors when someone else does it?

Of course, the exact metrics that your business needs to consider may not be on this list, or you may only need to monitor some of the items on this list. The metrics you measure may be different; the fact that you need to have metrics is common to all businesses.

Learn to Define Better Business Objectives

Once you begin to speak and understand the language of numbers, start to test and measure key metrics in your business; you can then also review your business objectives to ensure they are SMART: Specific, Measurable, Achievable, Results-oriented and Time-bound.

Specific: Your objectives should spell out exactly what you want to achieve and how you want to achieve it. The more specific, the better.

Measurable: They should have distinct criteria which allow you to measure your progress and determine the success of your work. This is perhaps the most critical factor for determining what risks you should be taking.

Achievable: While you should be aiming for the stars, and your goals should challenge you, you also need to make sure your goals make sense and can be achieved. There's nothing worse for motivation than to have constant unattainable goals.

Results-oriented: This means that your goals should be about producing results. There's no point having goals that don't relate to the success of your business.

Time-bound: When you don't put a time frame on your objectives, they can sit at the bottom of your list forever. Remember, a goal without a timeline is just a dream.

When you craft your goals to be SMART, then it becomes clear what kind of direction your business needs to take – and where it needs to take risks.

Successful business owners don't leave their business up to chance. They follow fundamental principles that allow them to manage and improve their probability of success.

Increasing the probability of success on a project from 10% to 15% is a 50% increase! Colouring by numbers is perhaps not as much fun as colouring with no restrictions. But if it led to a 50% increase in your success on everything, would it be worth it?

How Ansoff Did It

"The essence of strategy is choosing what not to do."

Michael Porter

Igor Ansoff, a Russian-born mathematician and business manager, is often known as the father of strategic management. One of his seminal pieces of work has been the Ansoff growth matrix, a framework that is taught in most management institutions across the world today. In brief, the Ansoff growth matrix seeks to help businesses map strategic product market growth by honing in on developing products and/or markets.

The Ansoff Matrix has four alternative marketing strategies: Market Penetration, Product Development, Market Development, Diversification.

Market Penetration

Market Penetration is the most relevant for current products in an existing market. In this strategy, there can be further exploitation of the products without necessarily changing the product or the outlook of the product. This is often the lowest risk of the four strategies and often the attempt is to increase the number of transactions and conversion of leads and enquiries.

Product Development

Product Development focuses on either introducing new products to existing markets or modifying existing products. Typically, our average value based strategies revolve around developing or enhancing products and up-selling/cross-selling.

Market Development

Market Development or Market Extension involves the business moving to new markets with its current set of products. This can be done through segmenting the market, moving to new locations, franchising or setting up new distribution channels. This strategy assumes that the existing markets have been fully exploited. Clearly, this strategy is riskier and secondary to the previous strategies.

Diversification

Diversification involves marketing or selling new products to new markets at the same time. It is by far the riskiest of strategies as it involves two unknowns. Before starting to diversify, the business needs to have done a clear risk and return assessment.

Diversification could be related (within the same broad industry or sector) or unrelated (like the Virgin Group). This is often an attempt to build a portfolio of businesses and decrease overall risk for the business owners/shareholders.

The Business Relevance

The Ansoff Matrix helps the business owner identify which strategy makes the most sense. Working with businesses across industries, I've often found that the 'exciting' things to do are often fraught with risks and, more importantly, not the most profitable.

Most businesses would not figure in the 100 largest companies in their industry in their location. What that immediately points towards is that Market Penetration is likely to be by far the most useful and profitable strategy. The trouble often is that for an entrepreneur, doing more of the same thing is 'boring' and they yearn to start experimenting again.

As one of my mentors once told me, the most successful businesses focus on saturating their current market rather than expanding into new ones. It is satisfying to the ego to have a client in every part of the world but it is immensely more satisfying to have ten times the number of clients in a radius of ten miles from where you are – and often a lot more money in your pocket too.

Business owners keen to diversify and enter new markets often first need to go back to fundamentals to check how much of the current market has been penetrated by the business. For most businesses, the answer is usually less than 1%. If you do decide to pursue the riskier strategies, make sure they are not at the expense of the simpler and more profitable ones.

The £100,000 Dilemma

"Instead of saying 'I don't have time' try saying 'it's
not a priority' and see how that feels."

Laura Vanderkam

How much do you earn from your business per hour? And
how much do you charge out? Unless you are in a business
charging per hour, this might seem hard to know or even
irrelevant. And even if you do charge an hourly rate, chances
are that not all your hours are billable.

Most business owners never think of how much their time is
worth per hour. This leads to the fallacy that you save more
money in the business by doing stuff yourself and not hiring
an extra hand.

 Here's a simple calculation: if your profit after tax
(and before you take any money out of the business)
is £50,000 for the year and you are working 50-hour
weeks, with a couple of weeks of holiday every year, your per
hour rate is £20 (£50,000 ÷ 2,500).

Is £20/hour a rate you are happy to work at? If not, what
could you be doing to increase this rate? The answer is quite
simply in the mathematics: either increase the numerator
(increase the profitability of the business) or decrease the
denominator (decrease the number of hours you are spending
in the business).

The best way to increase the numerator is to simply look to do activities in which the per hour rate is significantly above £20.

If you went looking for and found a new key customer, how much will they be worth over the next few years? How many hours of work would that take and what is the difference on a per hour basis?

If you look at the value of time recruiting a new member of staff, training staff to be as good (and valuable) as you, what is the per hour return of this effort?

For most business owners, these are the all incredibly high-value activities – which often are put off as they are busy doing 'other stuff'! It's not rocket science – the higher the value of the work that the business owner does, the more profitable the company.

The best way to decrease the numerator is often to either re-allocate your time to non-business activities by drawing a hard line around your personal time or to begin to consciously stop doing lower per hour rate activities.

 Make a list of everything that you do on a daily, weekly, monthly, quarterly and one-off basis (head over to the Resources section of our website for a template to help you audit your activities).

Against each activity, write down what you could pay someone hourly to do this. If the hourly rate is less than you can be worth when doing your most valuable work, get someone to do the lower paid work – even if it is an outsourced freelancer.

Change your question from 'Can I afford to employ someone?' to 'Can I afford *not* to employ someone?' As a business owner, you have a remarkably high level of control over your income compared to employees. Why then would you choose to do low-wage work? You need to pay someone else to do the lower value work so that you can do the more valuable work and earn more money for the business.

Gay Hendricks in his book *The Big Leap* talks of how people need to spend as much of their time as possible working on their 'Ikigai' (reason for being) or their 'Zone of Genius'. If you focus on using more of your time to earning a higher rate per hour, your business will be more profitable or you'll be able to work fewer hours – whichever is more important to you and you are a lot more likely to be working in your 'Zone of Genius'.

Here's another thought: How much per hour would you pay for extra leisure time? How much per hour would your partner/child pay you for an hour of your leisure time? Is £20 per hour worth the sacrifices you make?

Business Lessons from Football

"Confidence doesn't come out of nowhere.
Confidence comes out of hours and days and weeks
and years of constant work and dedication."

Roger Thomas Staubach

Whichever club you support, there can be no debate that Arsene Wenger OBE has been one of the most successful and revolutionary managers in English Premier League history. Among the many aspects of his managerial style and philosophy transferable to the business setting, I believe that those below are the most crucial.

Hire Potential

"We do not buy superstars. We make them."

One of the major recurring themes of Arsene Wenger's tenure at Arsenal is that he does not rely on big-money transfers, but rather on spotting and obtaining youngsters with potential. For business owners, sometimes a focus on hiring people with the most experience makes us forget that a key criterion for success in teams is 'coachability' – something people who have 'been there, done that' may lack. Focusing on people you can train and mould, and someone who you can see grow with your business may be the secret weapon for your business. Combine this attitude with a robust recruitment process and you are set to fill your team with not only well-trained superstars, but incredibly loyal ones as well.

Know Your Budget

"My target is to make the players as rich as possible within the financial constraints of the club. My target is not to give them less money. I'm happy to make them rich."

A big factor of Wenger's success at Arsenal has been his tight control of the club's finances. Wenger has helped Arsenal Football Club through the financial rigours of moving into a new stadium, while keeping the club competitive at the highest level. For any business to be successful, it is extremely important to know your numbers and to keep a keen eye on all your finances. Spend well and spend wisely.

Do Not be Afraid to Stand Out

"The biggest things in life have been achieved by people who, at the start, we would have judged crazy."

To compete and succeed you sometimes need to stand out from the crowd. A business owner is essentially a problem solver. It is quite likely that the reason the problem still exists is that no one has come up with the right and differentiated solution that you can provide. In football, as in business, if you do what everyone else does, the best you can hope for is to be average, and the worst possibility is to be completely ignored. In a world where we have more choice than ever, you need to give people a reason to choose you.

Believe in Your Business

"If you do not believe you can do it then you have no chance at all."

Everything is created twice – first in your mind and then in reality. If you do not believe in yourself and in your products and services, why would anyone else? Wenger believes in his team, in his philosophy, and his process to succeed, because if he did not, he might as well just give up, especially when competing in the top leagues of European football. Your conviction flows into everything you do and has the potential to inspire or alienate your team.

Take a Break

"Any man who concentrates his energies totally on one passion is someone who hurts the people close to him."

Wenger is a true student of football, and that is where his passion lies, but he realises that if that was his sole focus, he would burn out and neglect those around him.

As a business owner, it can be easy for you to focus all your time and energy on your business and prioritise it above everything else in your life. Success in life and success in business are not the same thing. You need to work hard – no one can deny that – but you need to know when to take a break and take a step back from your business as well. Obsession in any form is unhealthy and may lead to a breakdown of personal relationships.

It is not hard to understand why Arsene Wenger is commonly referred to as Le Professeur, as his footballing knowledge is only second to his business acumen. Even if you are not a big football fan, there are lessons to be learnt from this managerial master in helping run a better business.

Now, one final lesson from a football player, turned economics student, turned football manager, and now a coach:

"Nobody has enough talent to live on talent alone. Even when you have talent, a life without work goes nowhere."

The 4Ds of Productivity

"One important key to success is self-confidence.
An important key to self-confidence is preparation."

Arthur Ashe

When was the last time you made a significant improvement to your time management habits? If your task list is extremely long and interspersed with items that have never really been important to you, you may be able to improve your personal productivity dramatically with a few changes.

There is a simple framework/productivity tool that may help you when it comes to organising and managing your task list.

The first thing you do is make a list of all the things that you need to do. This is a moving list, because there may be a few things that you didn't achieve so you move them to the next day or the next week because that is how life works. But the first step is to have a list of everything that needs doing.

The Default Diary Tasks

Before you go further in prioritising that list though, you must first identify the core, non-negotiable items. What is it on your list that absolutely must be done, otherwise the consequences will be truly dire?

These items you need to add to what we call your 'default diary'. That means simply going into your calendar and putting in a recurring item that happens every week for those items to happen. This works because now there is a specific time allocated to the activity. If you do not put that time into your calendar, and just leave it on your list, the chances are that it will slip. Finally, make sure that in some way or form, you are being held accountable through either calendar reminders or through your team reminding you.

The 4Ds Framework

Once you remove the non-negotiable activities, you are left with the tasks that you choose to do. And that is an important decision you make, because when you choose to do something, you are also choosing not to do something else.

I believe that after you make a list you need to be extremely selective in what you do from that list. It is not about hard work and doing everything. It is about knowing where to strike and what to focus on.

But the question is how do you choose what to do and what not to do? That is where the 4Ds framework comes in.

This framework is based around four ways that you can categorise any task you do:

- You can Do the task yourself
- You can Delegate the task to someone else
- You can Defer the task to another time
- You can Dump the task altogether

And the one question which helps you decide what to do with the task is: Do I need to do the task now?

Question 1: Do I **need to do** the task now?

This is the first thing you should ask yourself of any item because it is too easy to fill your list with unimportant and irrelevant items that make it very difficult to see your other tasks. Can you strike this task off your list? Is it there just because you like making long laundry lists?

You might realise that this task is not actually adding value to your business and not helping you move forwards towards the goals in your business plan, so it should be removed from your headspace.

What tasks are you doing that you should just dump?

Question 2: Do I need to do the task **now**?

If you really cannot strike the task off your list, then you need to ask yourself if this task needs to be done right away or not.

Is this something that can wait until next week, next month, or next quarter? Will it help the company to run better or move faster if it was done now?

What tasks on your list will not make a significant difference whether you do it sooner rather than later which you could Defer?

Question 3: Do I need to do the task now?

OK, so you really need to do this task today or this week, then you need to move up to the next step and ask yourself: Can somebody else do this?

Can you delegate this to a business partner or to a team member? Will someone else do this better than you, or will it empower someone else in your team to take on a role of greater responsibility in the business?

Learning how to delegate effectively is an important part of team management. If you are constantly thinking that it is better for you to do things yourself because it will be faster, then that is another problem altogether which may involve a broken team model. It is nearly impossible to achieve sustainable growth without a capable team supporting you.

What tasks on your list could you Delegate to someone else?

All Right, Just Do It

If you have moved through these three questions, then you have arrived at the work that must be done, must be done now and must be done by you. You then need to put aside the time in your diary for it, let it live and breathe in a place in your diary and just get on with it.

But if you ask yourself those three questions first, you will find that your 'Just Do It' list is not only a whole lot shorter, but is filled with things that are moving your business forward.

This is a questioning process that most senior leaders use – because they must! Wouldn't it be a lot more productive to adopt it even if you do not have to right now?

Your time is one of the most important assets in your business and it is important that you use it in activities that have the highest return for your business. If you can tie your own time efficiency to empowering your team with greater responsibilities, the benefits to your business are likely to multiply.

Get Paid Forever

"It is much easier to put existing resources to better use than to develop resources where they do not exist."

George Soros

There is a well-known 'secret' out there that not enough people grasp in its entirety: the concept of leverage – getting more done with less effort. Leverage works on constantly asking the question: What is the one thing I can do such that by doing it everything else will be easier or unnecessary?

Here are a few steps that can help you get real leverage in your business.

1. Stop Doing Everything Yourself

One of the key issues a business owner needs to address to begin using leverage is their own belief that they can do it all themselves. The belief that they are the superhero of their business, always at hand to solve every problem – until the day that they aren't.

For a lot of business owners, being good at something becomes the primary reason they do not become great. They continue to do the very thing that they are good at and refuse to compromise by letting someone else, someone who would not do the job as thoroughly as themselves, take on their tasks.

The first step is simply the decision to consciously change towards moving away from always 'doing' everything and allowing others to step in, even if they make mistakes.

2. Give Away Your Low-Skill, Low-Fun Tasks First

The Skill-Fun Matrix can be used to help people identify the things that they should stop doing.

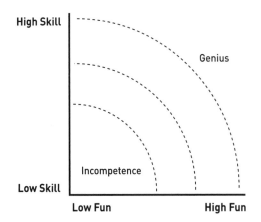

The initial tasks to delegate and the ones that give you the most leverage are the ones that sit in the low-fun and low-skill quadrant. If you don't enjoy doing something, unless it is business critical you are likely dragging your feet on it already, particularly if you do not have the skills required to do the task well.

They also have the potential for creating the most distractions – these tasks are those annoying buzzing flies in your work world which steer you away from the tasks where your true talent can shine.

In the end, you want most of the work you do to be in the High-Fun and High-Skill quadrant – that means picking off everything else and critically examining it to decide if it really needs to be done by you.

3. Match the Right Person to the Role

A cube-shaped peg may not go into a circular hole. With the ability to get the right person for the job, something you have as a business owner, rather than having to get the same people to do all the jobs, you release immediate potential into your business.

When trying to find a team member, you need to ensure they are *right* for the role that they're filling. Don't hire someone just because they are easy to hire. Before you start hiring, you must define the role along with the responsibilities and the desired output.

Ask yourself:

- Do they have the right skills for the job?
- Does their personality type match the tasks that they'll be doing?
- Are they enthusiastic about the job?

4. Delegate Work, But Don't Abdicate

Introducing a system is critical to any area where you want to create leverage. The most important of these systems in your business is often the process of managing your team.

As a leader, your tasks will either be tasks where you are doing, creating or 'making', or tasks where you are directing, assisting, delegating or 'managing'. The key to effective delegation is to ensure that you have time for managing as well as making.

There are a few simple ways to ensure you really 'lead' your team:

1. **Define the outcome.** You need to start off by ensuring your team members know exactly what is expected of them. The best way to do that is to tell them from the very beginning.

2. **Timeline everything.** If there's no urgency, tasks rarely get done. The easiest way to timeline activity is to start with when the result needs to be done and then backtrack over the steps that need to happen to get to that result, and how long those will take.

3. **Ask them to recap.** After you assign a task or project, always ask your team to repeat the task to you. Hear it in their words and make sure that they have understood and are on the same page as you.

4. **Include a touch point in your diary.** You must ensure that there is a point mid-way through a project where you check in and make sure everything is on track. If you wait until the end, then you may not catch issues before it's too late.

5. **Install a task management system.** There are several powerful task management systems out there such as Asana or Podio, which can take your task management to new heights. But in smaller companies, it can often be better to go simpler and use a basic spreadsheet to manage tasks.

 Go to the Resources section of our website to access a simple tool based on Google Spreadsheets that we use to keep everyone on track.

5. Document Everything You Do

One of the key steps in creating a system-based business is the creation of documentation to record how things are done in your business. If the 'right way' is in your head, you're going to remain trapped in doing the work too.

Pull that information out from your head and document it. And remember to keep it *simple*. No one is going to want to read reams of training material – and they probably won't absorb it.

Here are a few ways you can keep your documentation concise:

- Create one-page documents. Limit yourself to a page and you'll be amazed what you're able to condense.

- Use checklists and bullet points. We all operate much better when we've got a clear list of things that look and feel achievable.

- Create how-to videos either using a camera or using software that captures your screen. Videos are easier to digest for a lot of people, especially if you're explaining a technical process or steps to be taken in a process.

Concise and comprehensive documentation adds to your business by increasing the likelihood of a new hire being successful and ensuring your business runs without interruptions and the way you want it to.

If you want your business to work for you, instead of you constantly having to work for the business, you need to start thinking leverage and doing things that would get you paid not once but forever.

Swimming Naked

"You only find out who is swimming
naked when the tide goes out."

Warren Buffett

More businesses go bankrupt for lack of cash than for lack of profits. Often when the economy is doing well, businesses survive despite themselves; the margin of error is high enough to allow even businesses with bad processes to do well.

However, the moment the tide turns and there is a shock to the economy, the need to work harder and smarter becomes critical to survive and prosper. It is important therefore to remember that the biggest reason businesses fail is because they run out of cash.

The Cash Gap is a useful measure to understand why your business may be struggling with cash. Simply put, the Cash Gap refers to the time in days from when you take money out of your business (through purchase of stock, salary payments etc.) and when you get paid by your customers. The larger your Cash Gap, the more your bank balance is likely to be under pressure.

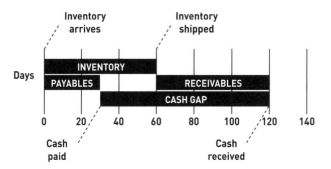

How could you decrease the Cash Gap in your business? Should you be paying your suppliers a little later than when you are paying them? Should you be following up for client receivables more rigorously? Should you be decreasing the amount of stock you keep in your business?

There is often an unnecessary amount of cash stuck in working capital creating the Cash Gap. Before you go to the bank for your next loan, re-evaluate how much money your own business could release – you may find that you don't really need the bank after all.

Under Your Nose

"I don't look to jump over 7-foot bars: I look around for 1-foot bars that I can step over."

Warren Buffet

As an outsider looking in at a business with cash flow issues, one of the first places I look is the debtors of the business and the process for collecting money due to the business.

The reason this is usually a neglected area in most businesses is that it is not exciting enough; a lot of entrepreneurs think of themselves as salespeople, not as money chasers. So they move on to the next sale and hope receivables will take care of itself.

The result is that usually the approach to chasing aged debtors is not very structured, ad hoc, not measured or targeted and, therefore, it is an activity that is only done as an afterthought. It's only when there is cash flow pressure that the business owner sits down with the team member in the accounts team and asks, "What's going on? Show me what's pending." And panicked follow-up ensues often accompanied by stress for the team, stress for the business owner and, critically, stress for the customer relationship.

What if we had a way to turn the process around to become more proactive? What if there were a few things that you could implement right now that could get the system working for you again and again? Guess what, there is a process and there are a few things you could do to get started right now.

Your Terms of Trade – Don't Be Someone Else's Bank!

What are your Terms of Trade? Do you give 30-day credit by default to all customers simply because that is what the accountant has set up on your invoicing system? Why is it not 21 days or 14 days? Do you have the same credit terms for all your customers? What would happen if you changed the default to 7-day credit? How many exceptions to the rule would you need to allow? You don't know what you don't know and you need to at least ask the questions to see what answers come from there.

You are a bank to your debtors – the clients who you have worked for/supplied to but who've not paid you yet (just as your creditors and suppliers are potentially lenders to you). The only difference, of course, is that the money you are lending is at 0%!

What if this cash flow was sitting in your business so you could choose to deploy it in the right direction – marketing, investment or hiring?

So, the first step is simply to improve your terms of trade – even if only for some clients.

Build Your Outstanding Table

Now this should be familiar to most business owners as this is typically an easy report that most businesses generate either on a weekly or monthly basis. This lists the total outstanding, then you have a few brackets for days that the money has been outstanding: 0-30, 31-60, 61-90, >90 days.

 Let's take an example – £100,000 is outstanding in the business:

Days	0 – 30	31 – 60	61 – 90	> 90 days
£ Outstanding	£40,000	£30,000	£20,000	£10,000

The first thing you need to start doing is measuring the current percentage split that you are seeing as far as this outstanding is concerned. So in this example that table would change to:

Days	0 – 30	31 – 60	61 – 90	> 90 days
£ Outstanding	£40,000	£30,000	£20,000	£10,000
% Outstanding	40%	30%	20%	10%

Here's an important distinction you need to make at this stage. The customers who have not paid you for more than 60 days have the potential of directly impacting your profitability. Even if they do love you, the probability of them paying you is getting slimmer and slimmer and that is a concern. The first two columns are in fact your cash flow buckets. A customer that moves from 15 days outstanding to 30 days or 40 days has the potential of having a significant impact on your cash flow.

The first two columns therefore impact cash flow whereas the last two columns impact profitability and both are critical.

Set Your Targets

Here's the one simple technique you need to implement: you need to set targets – not to decrease the overall outstanding figure but a percentage decrease in each section. Remember, having more outstanding is often a sign of growth of your business; as you grow, you will invoice more, your customers will be more and this amount will go up.

Your table with targets will look something like the following:

Days	0 – 30	31 – 60	61 – 90	> 90 days
£ Outstanding	£40,000	£30,000	£20,000	£10,000
% Outstanding	40%	30%	20%	10%
% Target	60%	33%	5%	2%

By setting a % target, you've neutralised the impact of growing sales and focused efforts on ensuring that the focus is on decreasing the outstanding that is more dated.

Decide Who To Chase

The next step is to look through the list of clients with amounts due for a longer period. At this stage, however, you're looking for large absolute amounts. There is often a tendency at this stage, especially in team members, to focus on activity – tick boxes confirming that all customers have been followed up. The important focus the business owner needs to bring in at this stage is the focus on the places where the biggest impact would be. Eat the frog – spend most of your time chasing customers who are holding on to the bigger amounts; this is not a clean-up and tidying exercise, it is a quest for cash.

Look through the list of clients with outstanding in the 31 – 60 column. Again, which customers have the largest amounts in this bracket and for how long now have they have been outstanding? If they are close to 60 days, your alarm bells should be ringing. You should be acting on it a lot faster because hopefully you will be reviewing this whole figure set every month, if not every week.

Systemise

Don't stop yet. The final lap here is the bit which is not urgent but important to ensure you are building your business asset. Document and systemise the process and identify the person in your team responsible and accountable for making it happen regularly.

Single Point of Failure

"I won't say we have to win. I won't put that
pressure. But we can't lose."

José Mourinho

Countless entrepreneurs dream of creating a successful venture, selling it, and sailing off into the sunset. What is surprising, however, is that the amount of thought and effort that is put into something that usually happens just once in an entrepreneur's lifetime is often shockingly minimal.

When you sell your product or service, you don't sit around waiting for someone to come knocking and then jump at the first offer. You polish the product or service, make it match the exact need that you are trying to solve and then go out rigorously looking for the right buyers.

In my experience, to ensure you generate the best value for your business at the point of sale, you need to start the work of preparing your business for sale at least three years prior to going out to sell. Even if you never want to sell your business, it is good practice to think of a sale as a goal for the business as it clarifies a lot of things that really add value to the business.

There are quite a few things that can work towards improving the value of your business. However, I find that the ones listed below have the maximum impact.

1. Reduce Customer Concentration

You need to ensure that no single customer accounts for more than 10% of your cash flow and profitability. When you rely on a low number of customers, the risks associated with your business increase. A large account may be attractive in the short term but significantly increases the risk associated with the business. Strive to spread your cash flow concentration thinner and hedge your bets on more than just one or two main clients. If you are unable to do this, make sure you protect your revenue by creating layers through signing contracts and officialising agreements you have in place with your customers.

2. Product Rationalisation

Having an uncontrollable and unprofitable range of products (or SKUs – Stock-Keeping Units) often leads to a decrease of your profit margins. Reduce your high-volume, low-margin stock and consolidate your most profitable products. By concentrating your efforts on a controllable number of goods (with none of them accounting for more than 10% of your revenue and profitability), you increase the sustainability of your business while making it easier to systemise.

3. Review Marketing Activities

Review all your marketing and advertising activities to ensure that you are getting the highest return on these investments and you are not making any glaring errors. If you do not have the processes in place to measure such activities, this is the best time to develop them. When you have a clear picture of how your marketing is performing, consolidate your marketing investments, review, and optimise. Ensure you are not spending money that you could be showing in your bottom line in activities that do not lead to an increase in the top line.

4. Reduce Your Costs

The value of a business is directly related to the profit it makes and has the potential of making. Managing your costs and increasing your margins therefore has a direct correlation to the value of your business. Review all your fixed and variable costs to ensure that your margins are as healthy as they can be. Empower your managers and employees to explore and highlight where the company might be overspending. After conducting your reviews, enforce discipline in expenditure by outlining how much and on what each department should be spending moving forward. Create accountability within your workforce and align incentive structures as closely to profitability as possible.

5. Efficiency Through Processes

One of the biggest concerns any potential buyer has is whether the business would run without you, the business owner. Without you at the helm of the organisation, uncertainty could potentially spread through the business. Remember that a truly successful business is a profitable one that can run without you. This is where leverage through systems and processes comes into place. Ensure that your processes are such that your team runs the business on the back of the systems that you have helped create. Take the time to review and develop your current processes, create new ones, and most importantly, document them.

6. Employees Can Make or Break Any Company

High employee turnover is one of the biggest worries that new owners are likely to have when buying a business. Without experienced employees, the stability of the company may be called into question, as years of know-how and specific skillsets will have just walked out of the door. To build your company's value, you should have a high-quality workforce that is loyal not just to you but to the company. Besides ensuring that you hire the right type of people in the first place, you need to give them a reason to stay. Incentivise your employees with long-term rewards attached to the company's success, such as incentive plans based on value added in the business or business profitability. Always know who your key employees are and ensure that you have clear transition foundations laid out to assist with the uncertainty that will undoubtedly result from a change of ownership.

7. Tidy Up The Business

First impressions, even when buying a business, truly do matter. The first thing which potential buyers will notice will not be your business model or your processes, but your business's physical structure. Prior to any sale, make sure that your office, factory, warehouse, machinery, etc. are looking their very best. Just like any open house, make your business look spotless and you will be starting off on the right foot. This may seem like a simple and superficial element; however, people at all levels make decisions based on emotion and first impressions make a big difference

As an entrepreneur, you devote a large part of your life in building your business. Make sure that when you let someone else take the wheel, you give your creation every chance it must remain great.

Each of the above has the potential of becoming a Single Point of Failure for your business sale. Ensure you address these and give your business the ability to continue your legacy.

The Success Trap

"When I'm old and dying, I plan to look back on my life and say
'wow, that was an adventure,' not 'wow, I sure felt safe.'"

Tom Preston-Werner

Several of our clients have come to us when they have already
been running for over 10 years. This may seem odd – why
would a successful business like that need coaching, right?
What's happening is that they are following the 10/5 rule for
continued business success, and are not quite sure at what
stage they have become stuck.

The 10/5 rule states that if you have been in business for 10
years or more and the business is not making revenue of more
than £5 million, you may need to rethink your organisational
structure and practices if you want to ensure that your
business continues to grow in the following 10 years.

At this point, successful businesses often become a victim
of their own success: being good at what they do has meant
they have become used to a certain way of running things.
However, a significant number of practices that have taken
entrepreneurs from start-up to success are simply unviable for
growing to a larger size, and many business owners refuse to
acknowledge that they have hit this point, sometimes called
the 'complexity ceiling'.

As a business owner, one of the things you need to recognise is
that 'what got you here won't get you there' – your practices
need to be adjusted if you want to take your business to the
next level. With businesses coming in all shapes and sizes,

there is no single textbook that has all the answers to business success. However, most businesses do experience a common set of roadblocks and hurdles during specific stages of their development, so it is important to recognise what stage your business is at.

The five stages model showcases the key characteristics and warnings at each of these stages and makes you re-evaluate the changes you need to make to your business structure.

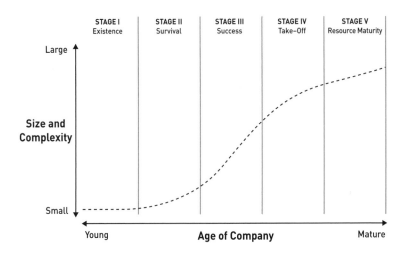

STAGE I Existence

At this start-up stage, the organisation is a simple one whereby the key focus is staying alive – which is easier said than done as more than half of the businesses that start every year fail in their first five years. Furthermore, the owner of the business is usually the whole operation, performing all the most important tasks themselves.

The key points that these businesses must focus on are attracting new customers, fulfilling demand as it comes in, and providing a product or service of a higher quality than their competitors.

STAGE II Survival

Once a business breaks through from the existence stage, they will be evolving into an organisation which focuses on revenue and cost management, rather than just staying afloat. The owner is also still in a hands-on role as the organisational structure remains very simple. Many business management consultants agree that the major change between the first two stages is the business's mindset, which has moved from asking if it can stay afloat to how it will look to grow.

The main pressure point that arises at this stage is usually a lack of revenue management strategy, which could lead to the deterioration of the business's profits and its ability to grow. Ask yourself how you will get the necessary cash flow for your business goals, and once you achieve it, how you will use it to maximise your business's potential.

STAGE III Success

If a business can manage the second stage well by generating and managing their income in a profitable manner, it will progress to Stage III – Success. This is a counterintuitively dangerous stage for a business owner and this is the stage that most business owners get stuck at – and where they need to think about applying the 10/5 rule.

At this point the business is healthy in its ability to generate cash flow and is beginning to integrate efficient processes within the organisation. The organisational structure at this point is becoming slightly more decentralised with the introduction of managers and junior level employees, meaning that owners should be able to occupy a more supervisory role. During the Success stage, the main concern is that there are two directions in which the business can go. Firstly, when experiencing success in a venture, an owner could decide to disengage from the business. This means that their major focus is to set a strategy to maintain the business's performance and revenue stream. In this direction, the owner will use the company as a source of support for external ventures, rather than looking to develop it. The second option for an owner at the Success stage is growth.

In this case, they will look to grow the company by consolidating its resources and risking it in their bid to realise the business's greater potential. Either of these directions requires that the business owner steps up and out of the hands-on daily operations and learns how to work on the business rather than in it.

This means they need to learn how to change their practices since, up until this stage, their own personal work was what kept the company going. At this point, it is time to create systems that allow it to run and/or grow without their constant supervision.

STAGE IV Take-Off

During this stage, the organisation is even more decentralised, with an increased hierarchical structure. Furthermore, the company's systems and processes have become more efficient, allowing managers to focus more on operational and strategic planning activities. Additionally, the owner's participation in the everyday working of the business is very minor, but they are still pivotal in setting its future direction.

There are two key potential problem areas for a business in this stage. Firstly, is the owner able to delegate tasks effectively to his managers? And secondly, are the revenue and expense controls in place, adequate to ensure that the business has the resources to satisfy the demands which growth brings?

It is critical that the correct systems and processes have been implemented before getting to this stage. Without that, the business quickly slides back from take-off into a position where the business owner must dive in and fight fires. The worst possible scenario is when a business goes from success to take-off and then descends right back down to survival because the organisational infrastructure was not there to support the rapid growth.

STAGE V Resource Maturity

At the fifth stage, the business is highly decentralised, and has the resources, as well as the expertise, to undertake detailed planning in an operational and strategic sense.

Furthermore, the processes and systems in place have been well integrated into the organisation, which allows the owner to fully separate himself/herself from the business. However, the business should not rest on its laurels here. At any point, the business could slide back into an earlier stage, so entrepreneurial spirit must be retained to build on its success.

The main concern of the business in stage 5 is that it needs to ensure it remains flexible and can pivot easily as a business, while also expanding its management force to meet the rigorous demands of the growing customer base. It is about creating systems and processes that flow efficiently, without creating unnecessary bureaucracy.

The rate at which businesses grow is dependent on a multitude of factors – from the industry you operate in, to the kind of managers you hire, and the quality of the products and services you offer. However, often, successful ventures go through the five stages above in some way, shape or form. If you do not fulfil the 10/5 rule, you are probably stuck at one of these stages – most often Stage III.

You need to identify at which stage your business has got stuck, understand what your next developmental stage is, and then take steps in changing your organisation to allow for you to access the next stage. You need to understand that what got you to where you are today will not get you to where you want to be in the future – it is time to adapt.

What stage are you at?

And the Winner is

"The greatest enemy of knowledge is not ignorance;
it is the illusion of knowledge."

Daniel J Boorstin

The language of business is one of numbers, and is therefore a language that every business owner should understand. When you know the numbers in your business, you can make smart, calculated decisions to move your business in the right direction. A critical distinction where I've seen many business owners making errors, especially when they are considering discounting their product, is the difference between margin and mark-up.

Getting these two terms mixed up – or thinking they are the same thing – can result in some big losses. You can use either, if you understand the difference. For the examples below, and for the sake of simplicity, I have assumed we are setting the price of a product.

Calculating Mark-up

 This is often the popular choice for a lot of retailers as it is a simpler calculation.

If the cost of the goods (material/ingredients) from the supplier is £100 and you want to mark it up by 60%, the price you will sell the product at will simply be £160. For a lot of retailers, marking up to two or three times the cost is the easiest way to keep their head around the numbers. Marking up to two times is simply a 100% mark-up: the price you will sell the product for will be £200.

Mark-up is applied to the cost of goods. The equation for how to calculate your marked-up price is: Marked Up Price = Cost of Goods x (1 + Mark-up %)

So, for the initial example: Marked Up Price = £100 x (1 + 60%) = £160

Calculating Margin

 When thinking of increasing the profit of a business, we usually discuss increasing the margin of the business. If we want to achieve a 60% margin, selling at a 60% mark-up is not going to cut it. The key difference is that margin uses sales as a denominator instead of cost of sales.

The equation for calculating gross margin is: Gross Margin% = (Sales – Cost of Goods) / Sales and re-arranging this, the equation to calculate your price at a certain gross margin is:

Price = Cost of Goods / (1 – Gross Margin%)

So, for the initial example, Price = £100 / (1 – 60%) = £250

As you can see, a 60% margin yields a very different price point compared to a 60% mark-up. Running at a 60% mark-up could mean that you are not making the amount of money you need to make in your business – and probably why you are also struggling to understand why the money you make seems to keep disappearing.

The problem usually is when business owners think: I need to achieve a 60% margin, so let me mark up my prices by 60%. What this does, of course, is significantly cut into your profits even before you have started. In the above example, at a 60%

mark-up, the price is £160 which really translates to a margin of 37.5% not the 60% that you originally intended.

Learning this language of numbers is not nearly as complicated as most people think. If you do want to play the game of business, it does make sense to play it as a professional and not as an amateur. And you cannot be a professional unless you master the language of numbers and begin to use it to your advantage to create massive results for your business.

Part III:
Mission

"You have to dream before your dreams can come true."

Dr APJ Abdul Kalam

You Are a Boat

"You don't know what you don't know. Confidence is
ignorance. If you're feeling cocky, it's because there's
something you don't know."

Eoin Colfer

What's the difference between an employee and a business
owner?

The analogy that I most relate to is that employees are like
trains and business owners are like boats.

A Train

A train has a powerful engine and is a solid mode of
transportation. For a train to reach its destination successfully,
we need a few things in place.

- First – we need to know where the destination is

- Second – we need to have a set of very clear tracks for
  it to reach from point A to point B

- Third – we need to make sure we have the right driver,
  conductor, linesman, station master and signalman on
  the train or along the track

- Fourth – we need to have the right junctions, refuelling
  stations and rest stops

None of the people who work on the train are usually
responsible for the big picture. They are skilled at what they
do but they need to have each of the above set for themselves
– they would not create these.

Let's apply this to your employees and team members.

- What level of clarity have you given to your team as to what your destination is? Are you expecting them to decide where the train goes?

- How clear are the systems and structures that need to be followed to reach point B? Are you expecting them to lay the tracks?

- How much training is given to each person in your team to make sure you move at the right speed and handle any issues that come up in the journey?

- What frequent reviews does your team go through – to guide them, motivate them, refocus and refuel them? Are you expecting to run a long-haul journey without a break?

These are the questions you need to ask yourself to get your team working more effectively, to make this machine, this engine, work with the right level of efficiency.

A Boat

Now let's talk about boats – business owners are boats. If you think about a boat in the sea and its tracks, the whole sea is its tracks. There is no set path and the boat does not really have a direction until or unless you as a business owner give this boat a direction – something that needs to be done again and again.

Now if you want this boat to move from point A to point B in this vast sea with winds and with waves and all kinds of climates and external factors, the first thing again is that you as a business owner need to be very clear as to where the destination is. Where do you want to take this boat to? Otherwise it can just bob up and down in the sea, and you can enjoy it for some time but after a point it will get very boring. You want to move forward, go places.

The second thing is that for the boat to move forward, you need to harness external factors – the opportunities out there which need your sail to be up. Your sail in a business sense is your goals, your dreams, what you are trying to achieve – the bigger the sail, the better it is to harness opportunities and move faster.

The third thing is a boat is likely to go a lot slower, if it moves at all, with an anchor holding it back. Anchors in businesses are past experiences and baggage which hold you back from achieving the results that the business is capable of. Sometimes these are identity/mindset related and sometimes they are simply a result of working with the wrong frameworks/models.

Essentially, it's about being in the sea, being in the unknown world, enjoying that adventure but also moving forward with harnessing the winds and the waves and letting go the anchors.

So, ask yourself: How much are you enjoying your business at this point? What do you need to stop doing? What do you need to start doing, as far as your employees are concerned and you as a boat are concerned? Are you expecting your team to be boats and your own business life to be a train?

Here's an old story on why being a leader is important, even if you are unsure yourself.

There was once a famous ship's captain, very successful at guiding merchant ships all over the world. Never did stormy seas or pirates get the better of him. He was admired by his crew and by other seafarers and captains.

There was one strange thing about him though. Every morning, he would lock himself in his quarters and open a small safe. In the safe was a small piece of paper which he would stare at for a minute before locking it up again and starting his day.

This went on for years and naturally everyone was quite curious about what this paper was. Was it a treasure map? Was it a letter from a long-lost love? No one ever dared ask him.

One day, the captain died at sea. After laying the body to rest, the first mate could not resist the suspense anymore and went to the captain's quarters to open the safe.

As he looked at the piece of paper, he turned pale. There were just four words on the piece of paper:

Port Left

Starboard Right

Climbing Everest

"Because it's there!"

George Mallory in response to the question:

"Why do you want to climb Mount Everest?"

Assume for a moment that you decide to climb Mount Everest. The first thing you would need to know is how high it is – 8,848 metres. This is usually where most people would give up the idea and get on with their daily lives.

What if you knew the secret recipe to climb 8,848 metres? Would that help? Would it make the trip less difficult?

Now think about a ladder exactly 12.12 metres high. Do you think you could climb this? Could you climb this again tomorrow? How about every day next week? Next month? Next year? With perhaps a bit of help from a friend or a coach, most people could do this.

Now consider this: if you climb this ladder every day for two years, at the end of the two years you would have climbed exactly 8,848 metres, the height of the tallest mountain in the world.

So, what happened here? Did the height decrease? Did the secret recipe help?

By breaking it into bite-sized pieces, the unachievable, even absurd target suddenly became quite achievable. The only trick then is to set the goal and start putting a foot on the next leg of the ladder, consistently, over two years. Knowing this neat little trick, however, is only about 10% of the battle. There are scores of people who decide to stop at different levels of the mountain, either satisfied with the 'progress' they have made or giving up the battle altogether.

As a business coach, one of my primary responsibilities is to define alongside my clients their Mount Everest, break it down to five-year, three-year, one-year and 90-day plans, and then work with them weekly to make sure we keep putting one step in front of the other. Sometimes, when I sit down with a business owner and help them define their BHAG (Big, Hairy, Audacious Goal), they think I'm being naive in my understanding of their industry, their competition, their products and services, their environment etc. etc. They are convinced that the audacious goal we are defining together is not possible. And often, they have 20+ years of industry experience to prove exactly that.

Most people overestimate what they can achieve in one year and underestimate what they can achieve in five years.

I may not be an expert in every industry, but I most certainly know how to set aggressive goals and help business owners achieve them. Of course, now you know the secret too. Usually, when broken down into bite-sized goals, it is surprising what you can really achieve in your business if you are fully committed to your goal.

Massive success in your business is 'there'. You just need to decide to go 'there'.

Everything You Know Could Be Wrong

"When the facts change, I change my mind. What do you do, Sir?"

Quote often attributed to John Maynard Keynes

I'm an avid believer in the importance of setting goals and following through with them. There is some extremely interesting work by Michael Neill which peels a further layer off how people could and should set goals. Michael breaks down our usual goal-setting habits into two broad components:

The first is mental and physical involvement – the extent to which we put our creative and physical energies into the pursuit of a goal.

The other is emotional investment – the extent to which we put our happiness, self-worth and wellbeing on the line in our pursuit of a goal.

We can choose to have higher or lower involvement and similarly higher or lower investment in every goal that we set.

Here's a framework to help understand this:

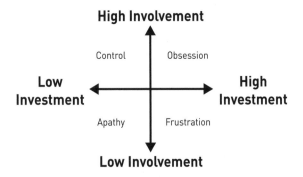

Low Investment/Low Involvement

This is when you don't particularly care what happens and are also not doing anything to move towards your goals. A person who doesn't care about how well their business performs will be unaffected by the trials and tribulations most entrepreneurs go through. He/she is also unlikely to do anything to change the situation.

Choosing this strategy is an extremely low-stress and relatively easy way to exist. Unfortunately, not only do you miss out on the fun of creation but also undermine the potential impact you could be having in your life and in the world.

High Investment/Low Involvement

This is the realm of the ardent sports fans and the moral pundits. If you follow any sport, you will recognise the emotions associated with watching a match or game and at the same time watching our own emotions go through a roller coaster as our team does well or not so well. Usually, besides cheering our heart out (or praying perhaps), there is little we can do to affect the result of the game.

This is a primary example of a situation where we care too much but have little ability to 'do' anything about it.

However, often our lack of real action boils down purely to our bad habits and our reluctance to take ownership of our situation. We get invested emotionally and realise that there is so much that requires to happen that we shock ourselves into helplessness and, feeling overwhelmed, do nothing.

High Investment/High Involvement

This is the mantra you hear from most motivational gurus. Work long hours, take massive action, do whatever it takes! And enjoy the emotional roller coaster through the thrill of winning and the agony of defeat.

For a person approaching life with this strategy, one minute they're on top of the world and the next they are down in the pits of despair. In fact, how they feel is dependent entirely on which point of the roller coaster ride they are on when you speak to them.

While this is often a very effective short-term approach, it often leads directly to burn-outs and broken families and often even scares people from setting any more goals for themselves.

Low Investment/High Involvement

Now what if you could choose to combine the best of both worlds – low emotional investment but high activities and involvement? There are two simple principles to help you do exactly that:

1. Identify which things are in your 'Circle of Control', which are in your 'Circle of Influence' and which are in your 'Circle of Concern'.

2. Begin to remind yourself consistently that your happiness and wellbeing is not out there at the end of a rainbow but right here regardless of what happens and how things turn out.

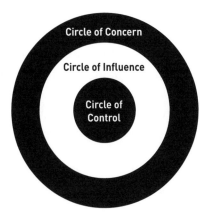

Decide to do anything and everything required to achieve your goals but be gentle on yourself when things do not turn out the way they should – especially when these results are outside your 'Circle of Control'.

This approach allows you to have all the excitement of being fully engaged in what you do without any of the stress of being emotionally invested. You do not need to continue taking pit stops to refuel your emotional tanks and can keep going consistently.

In summary, an old story comes to mind.

Once a wise old cat saw a small kitten running around in circles chasing its tail. He asked, "Why are you chasing your tail, little kitten?"

The kitten replied, "I've been attending cat philosophy school and I've learnt that the most important thing for a cat is happiness, and that happiness is my tail. Therefore, I am chasing it and when I catch it, I shall have happiness forever."

The wise old cat smiled and said, "Little kitten, I wasn't lucky enough to go to school, but as I've gone through life, I too have realised that the most important thing for a cat is happiness, and indeed that happiness is in my tail. The difference I've found though is that whenever I chase after it, it keeps running away from me, but when I go about my business and live my life, it just seems to follow after me wherever I go."

Often by letting go of trying to control the uncontrollable, we increase our influence and make meeting our goals a lot easier.

The Only Measurable Success Factor

"It is never too late to be what you might have been."

T S Eliot

A study by the Kauffman Centre for Entrepreneurial Leadership indicates that companies with a written business plan have 50% greater sales growth and 12% higher gross profit margins than companies with no plans. Note that the study does not say a 'detailed' 100-page business plan, or even a 'good' business plan. It just looks at 'written down' plans. In my experience, writing down and reviewing your business plan on a regular basis significantly increases the chances of moving your business forward in the direction you want to take it in.

So why are there so many business owners who still do not have even a one-page written down business plan?

Business plans are for when you are starting up or when you apply for a loan

Your business plan should be far more important to you than just as evidence for an external body. More important than showing other people that you are worth investing in is the ability to convince yourself and keep on track towards your goals.

A good yearly practice is to take a day out towards the start or end of the year to sit down with your management team to think and plan for what the business wants to achieve in the year. You review together what has been learnt over the last year, how the business has performed and the reasons for activities that worked and activities that did not work.

Are you on the path to your long-term goal or have you strayed? Do you need to realign your team and your activities?

I know the plan, why should I write it down?

Often business owners get caught in the 'I'm just a small business' mentality. They do not realise that just thinking of themselves as a small business could be the reason they have remained that way. The moment you begin to think of your business as a 'big business in training', the answer to this question 'Should I have a written down business plan?' is clear.

Who else in a big business besides the CEO/owner needs to know where the business is headed and how?

Writing a business plan is not the end game; it is, however, one of the crucial pieces of the successful business jigsaw that you are trying to solve and is analogous to having the four corner pieces that define the boundaries of the puzzle.

Your business plan is the beginning of you setting up processes so that your business can run without you. If you're keeping the business plan in your head, you're never going to be able to step back and work on the business rather than in it.

It is not the business plan, it is my mindset that is the problem.

Model or mindset – which is more important? I've come across scores of business owners who are enamoured by the belief that if they improve their 'winning mindset' and keep repeating to themselves how the universe will conspire to help them achieve their goals, they will succeed and of course get incredibly rich in the process.

Then there are others, who have almost a depressing attitude: always focusing on the things they and their team do wrong – and they run incredibly successful businesses.

I'm a firm believer that, not accounting for luck, 80% of the game of business is down to the model, not the mindset of the business owner.

Often, when you are the one in charge of everything in your business, it can seem like the model and the mindset are one and the same. That is also when writing down the business plan – separating yourself from the business model – starts helping you identify what, if anything, needs to be fixed first.

My business changes every week, anything I write down is bound to be wrong

If your business plan becomes invalid every time your business has a few changes, you may be planning incorrectly. Your plan is not a wish list. It should have specific, measurable, achievable, realistic and time bound (SMART) goals. It should help you to assess your status, and how you fit into your industry, and help you plan your next steps when changes come along. It should be a blueprint of exactly what you are going to do and have specific strategies you are going to use to move towards your goals, despite the obstacles along the way.

And yes, there will always be things that happen which are unexpected (or low probability). That's why you need to continually review your core plan.

A business plan should not be looked at only as the result – a document that you produce – but as a process. There is often an incredible amount of value in sitting down and thinking about the plan alongside your management team. The business plan in this context may therefore only be a framework to evaluate how the business has done compared to what you expected it to do and how you would want to move towards the future you want to create.

Up

"As long as you are going to be thinking anyway, think big."

Donald Trump

Three men – an Employee, a Manager and a Business Owner – were faced with the same daunting challenge: climbing a huge mountain that stood before them.

The Employee gets out of bed, looks out of his window and stares up at the mountain looming before him for what seems to be an eternity, decides it is not worth the effort, then turns around and jumps back into bed.

The Manager gets out of bed, looks out of his window and sees the same mountain. He dresses, straps on his climbing boots and sets out to scale the mountain, but after a brief attempt, he finds the incline too steep, the task too arduous and the goal unrealistic, so he retires back to the safety of his home.

The Business Owner gets out of bed, looks out of his window and sees the same mountain as the other two men. He prepares himself for the climb based upon the best available information at the time. He straps on his climbing boots and begins his ascent. He doesn't get very far before he's faced with such frightful weather that he is unable to see where he is going and so retreats. Once the bad weather passes, the Business Owner renews his climb. He then comes to a very steep incline and finds that, with no other way round, he must go up this path to move forward.

Try as he may, he makes very little progress, sometimes even falling back down to the base of this steep section to where he had started. But every time he dusts himself off and sets out with renewed determination to get to the top. Finally, after numerous attempts and many falls, the Business Owner climbs this steep section and realises that he still has a long way to go to reach the top. With renewed confidence, he moves gradually up the mountain, ever aware of the perils that each step could bring as he ascends to the very top.

Finally, at long last, he reaches the top of the mountain. Before he has even the time to enjoy the triumph and exhilaration of his long, gruelling climb, he looks over the top of the mountain and what does he see?

Another mountain!!

The moral of the story is that we must do whatever it takes to be successful in our businesses. Sometimes it means doing extraordinary things and sometimes it means going back to the basics. The 'basics' are what got us here in the first place and enabled us to have the opportunity to continue to 'climb this mountain' and reach the top. Yet sometimes we forget what got us here.

What got us here and enabled us to have the opportunity to do what we so passionately love to do is, first and foremost, the activities that are necessary to access and develop clients. Are we doing the *activities* that are necessary on a consistent basis to generate leads? Are we using all the various lead-generation strategies, testing and measuring what is working, and in such volume as to achieve a meaningful success rate? We should be increasing our allocation of time, energy and money into attracting more (and better) clients.

So, what are we doing now that is working? How have we modified our sales/marketing strategy to get clients now? If our lead-generation activity has slowed, what are we doing differently now that will create a different result? Are we maximising the opportunities we have with our existing clients both in terms of value provided to them and in gaining referrals? Are we continuing to build our database in targeted markets?

Remember, focus on the basics and meet your challenges head-on.

The 1% Goal

"Any intelligent fool can make things bigger
and more complex. It takes a touch of genius
and a lot of courage to move in the opposite
direction."

Albert Einstein

One of the key responsibilities of any business owner is to set goals – for themselves, for their business and for their team members. While most people recognise this responsibility, what they do not recognise is their responsibility to break down the goal into achievable chunks for their team members. This is critical to ensure that targets set are not perceived as unrealistic and even distressing to employees.

Remember that your team needs to be aligned 100% with what must be achieved because eventually they need to deliver and then manage the targets. Often, a target is perceived as unachievable simply because it is in aggregate. The moment you break down the goal into bite-sized pieces, suddenly everyone starts to believe in the smaller targets being achieved. Your responsibility then remains only to make sure that the small pieces come together to meet or even exceed your target.

The 1% goal is a handy technique to break down large goals.

Imagine a situation where you have set a goal for your business sales to increase by £500,000 over the next year. This could come across as a mammoth task to everyone, especially if you have never seen annual growth as high as this. Instead of inspiring the team, you will potentially have scared them. They will be already calculating the extra hours they must put in every week and the extra business they must bring on board. Within this environment where each team member is convinced that the target cannot be achieved, you will start by fighting against the tide of negative energy until, most likely, your team convinces you that the target itself was unrealistic.

Instead if you were to divide this goal as follows:

- Break the £500,000 goal into 1% goals of £5,000 each

- Break the 250 working days (approximately) in a year into 1%, that is 2.5 days

 Now, to achieve your target, you need to make £5,000 of additional sales every 2.5 days. If the £ value of your average sale is £500, that equates to ten new sales every 2.5 days (£5,000 ÷ £500) or four new sales every day (10 ÷ 2.5) to achieve your annual target. What you have done in the above 1% calculation is to turn the debate away from whether £500,000 additional sales can be achieved to whether your sales team and you can together sell an additional four items a day – a number that will often seem a lot more palatable. This will not only put less pressure on your team but also on yourself. When the leap from the 'now' to the 'then' is small then not only do things look more positive and achievable, the number of celebrations per goal achieved also increase manifold.

And it is a known fact that the more you celebrate success, the more it expands.

If your business target is an elephant, there is only one way to eat this elephant: one bite at a time!

Part IV:
Money

"Run for your life from any man who tells you that money is evil.
That sentence is the leper's bell of an approaching looter."

Ayn Rand

Blue Skin and Pointy Ears

"Good marketing makes the company look smart.
Great marketing makes the customer feel smart."

Joe Chernov

The film *Avatar* widely popularised the term that refers to a representative to such an extent that most of us still associate the word with the film.

The term 'avatar' is one we use to refer to a key concept in defining business marketing strategy. That is, identifying whom you are targeting – very precisely.

Why an Avatar?

Most business owners are already aware that defining the target market for your business is critical. It is one of the common questions we help our clients answer: How do I identify my target market?

We have often found that most business owners are not aware of how specific they need to be with this. For example, 'interior designers in London' may sound specific but is actually quite a *loose* target.

Try to think of it this way instead: marketing is not one to many, it's one to one, many times. What this means is you should not be marketing to an *audience*, but instead you should be communicating with an *individual*. And then you want to do that repeatedly.

So instead of trying to define a target market, you are trying to define a *target person* – your avatar. This is the person towards whom your marketing should be directed.

While your avatar may not have blue skin and pointy ears, you should be able to visualise them clearly and understand what would and would not work for them. You should be able to place yourself in their shoes and understand what drives their decisions. Once you do, then writing content, defining your channels, figuring out the designs of your website or marketing materials all becomes infinitely easier *and* more effective.

How to Choose An Avatar: The Six Essentials

Choosing an avatar requires a fair amount of structured thinking.

Your avatar sees the benefits and relevance of your products and services

This person should be your raving fan. Whatever the problem is that you are solving, you should solve it for this person and you should be the best solution that this person can think of. If your avatar loves you and what you do, then everything else becomes easier. They will convert more easily, they are more likely to come back again and again – every subsequent step becomes a lot easier.

Your avatar can be easily reached out to

For example, if you provide cleaning contract services you could choose a target person who is the head of operations in a good-sized corporate company, or you could choose the person in charge of operations at a school. Which one do you think is easier to reach out to? It may be easier to contact someone in the corporation – they are in a position that is designed to be contactable.

You must carefully consider how difficult it is to get in touch with your potential avatar, and factor that into your decision.

Your avatar is receptive to marketing

Going back to the cleaning contractor example, while it is easier to get in touch with someone at a corporation, they are less likely to be receptive to marketing. Corporate heads have marketing constantly thrown their way, while a school is less likely to get as much and will probably be more receptive.

Sometimes, your avatar may not be that receptive to your marketing – that is OK. The point here is to compare between your different avatars and, ideally, choose one that is more receptive.

Your avatar has a relatively short sales cycle

On a relative basis, you want to target someone where the time to go from initial enquiry to the purchase is as low as possible.

How short the sales cycle is depends on your business and the industry. Among your choices however, pay more heed to the target person with the shortest sales cycle.

Your avatar will buy more than once

You want your target person to buy from you repeatedly simply because it is often more difficult to continually go out looking for new clients who never come back.

This may not be the case for every business – some services are one-time only. However, with most businesses, it is a waste of your marketing spend if you are incurring all the costs to get a lead and they are only buying from you once.

Your marketing budget should be an investment, not a 'spend', and so when you make this investment, you want it to give you as much return as possible by increasing the number of transactions that a single converted lead makes.

This increases the lifetime value of your contact and therefore the return on investment on all marketing.

Your avatar spends a reasonable amount and makes you a good margin

Is your customer coming in and buying products or services from you that deliver value? Are they buying your products that have a high margin? Or are they only purchasing your peripheral products rather than your core ones? Do they only buy from you when you give them offers or put things on sale?

Remember, you should be segmenting your customers not just to identify their value, but also to determine how you approach them. Your target person should be a raving fan – which means they believe in what you are doing and are willing to pay for the quality products you are creating.

Your Avatar is Already a Customer

You may find that even after the previous exercises, your avatar may not yet be totally clear in your mind. This is likely because it is still someone you have imagined rather than someone that exists.

This next exercise is about taking everything you have learnt so far – about the essential qualities of your avatar and your imagined avatar – and applying it.

Step 1

Retrieve a complete list of your customers. Choose the customers that you already actually like. Would you want to have a coffee or a drink with them?

Step 2

Go through each of these favourite customers and start ranking them. Assess them based on the six essential qualities. Consider how much they match your ideal avatar.

Step 3

Choose your favourite (or maybe more than one favourite) and then actually interview them to get further details.

 We have an Ultimate Avatar Template in the Resources section of our website which you may want to use to ask the right questions.

Once you have those answers, you have a well-defined profile for your avatar that is built on real knowledge of an actual ideal customer.

Now you can start creating some marketing that is sharply directed at those people within your market who are an absolute perfect match for your business and product.

Customer is Not King!

"Darkness reigns at the foot of the lighthouse."

Japanese proverb

If you abide by the adage 'Customer is King', don't run a business – get a job as a customer care representative of one of our many banks. I'm sure they could use some help.

If, on the other hand, you recognise that 'bad customer' is not an oxymoron, then read on.

Not all customers are created equal and in our effort to make every customer delighted with our services, we often bend over backwards and sacrifice the basic purpose of the business: to create value for the business owner.

Most businesses can often subjectively define their bad customers: fickle, low paying, high maintenance and a drain on the time and resources of the company. There is, however, a very objective way in which the value of a customer to the business can be estimated.

 The Lifetime Value (LTV) of a customer is calculated as:

(Average Value of a Sale) x (Number of Repeat Transactions) x (Average Retention Time for a Typical Customer)

So, for instance, if there is a tutor whose pupil pays her an average sum of £50 per month and stays with her for two years then the pupil's LTV would be:

£50 x 12 x 2 = £1,200

Once you have the LTV of each customer in your business, you can immediately start categorising your good and bad customers. Clearly, a customer with high lifetime value is better than one with a low lifetime value. But a low lifetime value customer who uses up very few resources of the company is also a good customer.

The LTV should help you decide the optimal level of servicing for each client and even your promotion plans should be designed to attract the good customer with high LTV.

Once you have identified, subjectively and objectively, a bad customer, you can then start working on making the customer a better one – by increasing the average value paid, repeat transactions or retention. And sometimes, you may realise that losing this customer will allow you to focus a lot more on your high LTV customers, thereby increasing the potential returns to your business.

Before you crown your customers, make sure they are indeed the chosen ones.

The 20 – 80 Rule

"When it is useful to them, men can believe a theory
of which they know nothing more than its name."

Wilfredo Pareto

The Pareto Principle, also known as the 80-20 rule, is something that every business owner should keep at the back of their mind as they make decisions in their business. Simply put, the principle states that 80% of all effects come from 20% of the causes.

Unfortunately, the principle has been appropriated by efficiency pundits, and most thought around it avoids the hidden message of 'Massive Action Required' in the principle.

In sales, the application of the Pareto Principle means that for most businesses 80% of their sales revenue comes from 20% of their clients. More interestingly though, applying the opposite of this rule (the 20 – 80 Rule) to your prospecting can yield a good understanding of how many potential clients are going to enter your prospecting funnel based on the leads you reach out to.

Thus, if you target speaking to 100 qualified prospects every week, because according to this principle you will only reach 20% of your qualified prospects, your long list of qualified prospects needs to be 500 names (100 ÷ 20%).

Of the 100 qualified prospects you can speak to, only 20 will show any manner of interest and are potential clients. The remaining 80, no matter how good you are at selling, are simply not going to be interested.

Of the 20 who are now part of your sales process (yes, you do have a sales process, either deliberate or inadvertent), it is quite likely that 80% are going to drop off, for various reasons. Again, there is very little you can do about this except learn to accept it with equanimity.

These numbers may seem disheartening but this not-so-generous rule has left you with four clients who buy your product! But only if you made the rule stand on its head first and started with 'Massive Action' by increasing the size of your initial list by five times.

At first this may seem like a small reward for the effort put in, but understanding the principle can start laying the ground for how you are going to achieve your business and personal goals. Accepting the principle will also remind you not to take rejections personally as the more rejections you get, the closer you start getting to your 'Yes' prospect. Testing and measuring your conversion at every step of your sales process will ensure you can start to improve conversion rates through recognising bad practices.

The real difference between a good salesman and a bad one essentially boils down to the number of times they (or someone from their team) pick up the phone and speak to their prospective clients. Every other reason is merely statistical bias!

Risk Reversal

"Nothing is more fairly distributed than common sense;
no one thinks he needs more of it than he already has."

Rene Descartes

One of the biggest challenges in sales is when the customer is not quite convinced that your product or service is the right fit for them and they put off the decision to another time when they've thought about it a little more.

These 'maybe' customers have the potential of killing your business if you insist on relying on their coming back instead of working on your closing techniques. There is a proven way to overcome this common challenge – the 'puppy-dog close', a powerful way to engage prospects with your product, service or company – immediately.

The story of how this sales technique originated goes like this:

There was a very smart pet store owner who displayed his puppies in his store window. One day, a little boy, Bobby, was strolling along with his mother and stopped to look at and play with the puppies. The store owner asked if Bobby would like to hold the puppy.

"Oh, Mum, can I?" pleaded Bobby.

"OK, but only for a minute," his mother reluctantly agreed.

After more than a few minutes, Bobby's mother was ready to leave. Of course, Bobby didn't want to let go of the puppy.

"Bobby, that puppy really likes you too," the store owner said. "You know, I'm going to be closing up shop for the night, and this puppy is going to be here alone. Would you like to take him home for the night? If you don't like him, you can bring him back in the morning."

You know the end of the story. The puppy never went back to the store, and Bobby and his new puppy lived happily ever after.

The key idea that the store owner understood and took advantage of was the ability to identify the risk for his customer and overcome it by taking on some risk himself.

The catch in a 'risk reversal' strategy is that you need to take on more risk – but the secret is it's no risk at all. You're taking a calculated chance, one that you're near guaranteed to win.

In an average customer interaction, you usually ask the customer to bear the risk. They pay for a product or service and if it is defective, does not do what it says, or does not satisfy them in some way, they lose out. They are taking a chance with you, and with a history of slick salesmen and devious dealers shifting shoddy wares, the risk they are taking is quite real. You know the value and quality of your work, but they only know what you have told them, and they have learnt over time that they cannot trust most salespeople.

This becomes a 'barrier of entry' – a reason for the customer to not buy your product or service. This barrier of entry is what is standing between you and a dramatic sales increase.

So, lower the barrier of entry – reverse the risk.

The barrier is that the customer is worried that the product or service they are taking on may not be all they expect. The barrier is that they are taking a risk with you. So how do you lower the barrier? You take the risk away from them, and shoulder it yourself. You tell them that if they are not satisfied with your product or service, you will give them a full refund or replace the product.

Sounds like a risky move, right? What if people take advantage of you? What if they use the product or service for some time and then return it when they have got what they needed out of it? You would be left with nothing.

This is a legitimate fear. Even a possible scenario. But historical statistics tell us that for most products and services it is very improbable that your customers will return for the refund, and near-guaranteed that this approach increases your sales. This does not mean it will never happen – there will be people who ask for the refund. But the amount of additional business you will generate and close will far outweigh the loss due to the refund.

 Common scenarios working with companies that adopt a risk reversal strategy is that their percentage sales closed go up by almost 100% while the maximum refund we have ever seen given has been less than 5%. Looking through the numbers, if you can close one more sale from a potential 10 opportunities, increasing your sales by 10% from £100,000 to £110,000 and making a profit of £55,000 (at a 50% gross margin), you will have made an additional £5,000. If you have a 5% return rate, your cost of the strategy will be £110,000 x 5% x 50% = £2,750. You are still in the money! Even if you can't resell these returned products.

So, you are not really taking much of a risk at all. To the customer, it shows that you fully and completely believe in your product or service enough to take on the risk yourself – it proves to them that you can be trusted. If what you are doing is what you say you are doing, only the smallest percentage of people will ever likely demand a refund.

The best part is incorporating a risk reversal into your marketing and sales messages will cost you almost nothing: any benefit you gain comes at almost no cost.

If you are ready to experiment, there are different levels of risk reversal, so you can start lower in the hierarchy and work your way upwards.

Minimal Risk Reversal

This is where you burden some of the risk – for the things you essentially have control over. For example, if you were selling televisions, a partial risk reversal would be offering to replace or refund the television should it be found to be defective.

Full Risk Reversal

This is where you accept the burden beyond just the actual quality of the item. That means accepting if the customer is dissatisfied in any way at all, even if they just changed their mind. So, in the TV example, you would not just offer a refund if the television was defective, but if the customer was not satisfied in any way at all – even if it just did not 'look good' once they got it home.

More Than Full Risk Reversal

This is where you not only accept the full risk of the customer's dissatisfaction, but if they are dissatisfied, they leave with a little bit extra – for the inconvenience. So, in the TV example, you could offer the TV with a gift of, say, a voucher, and if the customer were to return the television, then you offer to refund the TV but let them keep the voucher. Get creative and increase the value of the offer!

Remember, although it seems like you might make a loss from the returns here, these tactics will increase your sales dramatically enough that any loss made will not impact your profits.

But you don't even need to take that as gospel – try it out! Start with a campaign that includes a Minimal Risk Reversal statement in it. Measure the results. Then try one with a Full Risk Reversal, then one with the More Than Full Risk Reversal. Test and Measure – that truly is the only real way to see what is going to work best for your company.

Would You Like Fries With That?

"I went into a McDonald's yesterday and said, 'I'd like some fries.' The girl at the counter said, 'Would you like some fries with that?'"

Jay Leno

A young salesperson once joined a big 'everything under one roof' department store in California. His first day on the job was rough but he got through it. As they were locking up, the manager came up to him and asked, "How many people did you sell to today?"

He responded, "One."

The manager said, "Just one? Our average salesperson sells to 20 – 30 people every day. How much was the sale for?"

The salesperson said, "$201,235."

Shocked, the manager asked, "$201,235! What did you sell?"

The salesperson responded, "Well, first I sold him a small fish hook. Then I sold him a medium fish hook. Then I sold him a large fish hook. Then I sold him a fishing rod. Then I asked him where he was going and he said he was going down to the coast. So, I told him he may want to look at some boats. We went down to the boat department and I sold him a twin-engine speedboat. Then we felt his Mercedes may not be able to pull the boat, so we went down to the auto department and I sold him a 4-wheel drive."

Amazed, the manager asked, "So the guy came in to buy a fish hook and you sold him a boat and an SUV?"

The salesperson responded, "Actually, he had come to buy a box of tampons for his wife and I said, 'Well, your weekend's shot, you may as well go fishing.'"

In my experience, businesses consistently ignore the most obvious and best strategies out there to increase their sales massively. One of these, working on increasing the Average £ Value, is used by almost every large company and yet businesses consistently turn a blind eye towards strategies that help them systematically do this.

Two of the most popular strategies to increase Average £ Value are Upselling and Cross-selling.

Upselling is suggesting your customer buys the more expensive model of the same product or service or that they add a feature that would make it more expensive. With upsell you are suggesting they pay more in exchange for a better product or service. Examples of this would be the customer buying a 50" TV instead of a 42" or buying a branded product instead of an unbranded one.

Cross-selling is when you suggest your customer buys additional products or services from a category that is different from the product or service they are purchasing. Examples of this would be buying a sound box to go with a TV or paper to go with a printer.

Here are a few quick tips on how you can start creating a system within your company to ensure cross-selling and upselling opportunities are not being lost.

Product Knowledge

Perhaps the most important aspect of increasing average £ value is to have robust product knowledge with everyone who delivers the product. How is this product used? What would make it easier to use this product? What need are customers trying to fulfil by buying this product? This helps the salesperson understand what other products fit well with this product in the customer's mind.

Price vs Perceived Value

An upsell works best when the perceived value of the product being upsold is significantly higher than the additional price that it commands. Remember, if the customer has already decided to buy a product, they have established an anchor for what they are willing to pay. Everything else is now going to be compared to this anchor price. Selling a £40,000 car to someone who has just test driven a £15,000 car may not work, whereas presenting a £16,500 car which is a sports model of the £15,000 car may just do the trick.

What Has the Customer Bought?

It's important to understand specifically what the customer has agreed to buy. What are the key features of the product that really convinced the customer? When trying to upsell, it is critical to maintain these key features. The upsell should add other reasons to buy and not attempt to replace the current reasons to buy!

Make Sure Your Team Knows the Key Cross-Selling Products

Some products work better than others for cross-sell. Everyone in your business needs to know what the specific cross-selling products associated with each product are. Think of your trip to the supermarket. You've done your shopping and you're ready to complete your purchase, and when you approach the payment aisle you see chocolate bars, magazines, chewing gum, mints all lined up tempting you. Cutlery, flowers and frozen peas would hardly make you reach out at this point.

Price Point

Cross-sell works better when the suggested items are half price or lower than the item being purchased. You'll have more success convincing a customer to add a £400 DVD player to a £10,000 car, compared to trying to cross-sell using a £2,000 custom finish. Cross-sell is also more effective when the original product is priced higher or requires more thought.

Take a quick look at Amazon to see how intrinsic these strategies are to the way they do business. If you're looking to buy a camera, you will be cross-sold at every step of the process: 'Frequently bought together' and 'Customers who bought this item also bought' when you first look at the product; 'Available warranties for this item' and 'Make this a gift' after you've chosen the product; and 'Amazon Prime' or 'Premium Delivery' when you're about to pay. You may also be upsold through 'More Buying Choices' right at the beginning.

Amazon reports that up to 30% – 40% of their sales come through cross-selling and upselling!

How much sales does your business generate through cross-selling and upselling?

Look at your own products and services and start to put these powerful average £ value strategies to work for you.

A, B, C and D Clients

"If you don't drive your business,
you will be driven out of business."

B C Forbes

Getting new customers is hard work and because most business owners recognise this, they spend an extraordinary amount of time and effort in getting new customers. The problem is that many business owners think that once they have a new customer, their work is over. Unfortunately, this is where their real work has only just begun!

When a prospect buys from you for the first time, they step on to the second rung of what in relationship marketing is called 'The Loyalty Ladder'.

The Loyalty Ladder

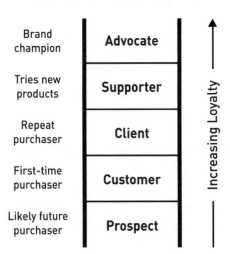

Brand champion	**Advocate**	
Tries new products	**Supporter**	Increasing Loyalty
Repeat purchaser	**Client**	
First-time purchaser	**Customer**	
Likely future purchaser	**Prospect**	

At this level on the ladder, there is very little customer loyalty and if a competitor comes along with a better proposal, customers are more than likely to give them a try, and you may never see that customer again.

The art of achieving a high level of customer loyalty is to move them further up the ladder, so that they become your brand champions and start soliciting customers for you. They will always buy from you, and in fact go a step further and start actively recommending other people to come to you, helping fill your sales pipeline.

So how do you turn your customers into advocates? The first step is to know who your customers are and categorise them based on how much they spend with you and how much of your time and resources they take up. You can do this by categorising all clients into A, B, C or D segments:

A = Awesome

B = Basically sound

C = Could do better

D = Don't want to deal with

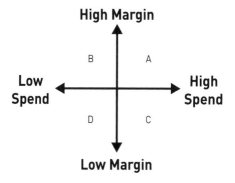

When segmenting your customers, make sure you are looking at their lifetime value and not just individual purchases. The lifetime value of your customer is simply the value the customer is going to contribute to your business over all their interactions with you. It includes the direct business that they provide you and the business that they get you through their referrals.

There is little point in spending time and effort with your D clients. These are the ones that haggle over price, take up your time over pointless queries and spend so little with you compared to the effort you put in that if you checked, you'd probably find that they bring you no profit at all. So just pass them on to one of your competitors!

C clients are those that have not yet been educated in how you like to do business. They have some of D's habits, but are profitable clients and are worth trying to upgrade. C customers are already doing good business with you. They are spending the money with you but you are not getting the returns you should be. Here you need to think of how you could generate operational efficiencies to increase the margins in your business.

B clients usually form the bread and butter of your business. Some you will be able to upgrade but others will need to be looked after and appreciated to maintain their loyalty. B customers are where you want to employ strategies that increase their spending. This may involve cross-selling or upselling strategies.

A clients are your advocates and raving fans. These people make what you do enjoyable. They not only buy from you but they will refer other people to you. These customers need robust relationship management – these are the ones you really want to stick around. Maybe you need to employ some loyalty strategies, maybe you just need to engage with them on a more regular basis.

Technology has made it easier for you to remain engaged with your customers. With email, blogging and social media, you can engage with customers as regularly as you like with very little investment. You could also use the more traditional methods of telephone calls, newsletters, direct mail and entertaining. Whichever method you use, you must bear in mind the appropriateness of the medium and its effectiveness and, most importantly, make sure that you consistently provide value to the customer.

While the likes of supermarkets have taken loyalty schemes to new highs, there are still some very simple strategies you can use that will have just as much effect. All you must do is monitor the level of business a client does and then reward them when they hit certain targets. This can be done via databases, accounts systems or plain and simple printed cards.

Rewards need not always be monetary – all you need to do is show perceived value. One great strategy is to find a non-competing business in the same sector and offer each other's clients something from your range, e.g. a photographer and a florist could swap a bouquet for a portrait. Remember that this will have the added advantage of putting a new person on to each other's loyalty ladder.

As you build up your portfolio of A clients, you will realise that you are in fact building one of the strongest legs of your business's sales and marketing machine.

Helping people climb the ladder.

There is of course no one-size-fits-all strategy when it comes to a business's customer relationship building. The activities that you use will be highly dependent on who your customers are, what your business does and what your business goals are.

There are, however, two things that you should consider when thinking of engaging your customers.

First, which segment of your customer base are you working on? Is this activity appropriate for that segment? If you are targeting B customers, then the activity you employ should be directly aimed at increasing their spend with you – such as upsell strategies via email marketing or social media.

However, if they were C customers, they are already spending with you – you don't need to sell to them, just get them more excited and enthusiastic. What you need to do is ensure you are consistently providing value so content marketing becomes more important.

Second, is the cost of applying the activity worth the benefit of moving the customer up the ladder? Look at the actual numbers – determine the acquisition costs involved in using the activity to take customers to the next level and compare this to the lifetime value that customer is contributing.

Split it! Segment it! Know which customers need what activation from you, what activation strategy is required, and what action is required. Essentially, if you can measure in a very concrete manner, you can manage better and you can improve. And that's the whole idea.

Not only is it easier to move people up the loyalty ladder compared to getting new people on the ladder, it is also a more sustainable way of doing business and therefore adds to the overall value of your business.

The Million Dollar Question

"There are no traffic jams along the extra mile."

Roger Staubach

How much should I spend on advertising?

Ideally, the answer is zero! You should invest, not spend money on advertising. Every pound invested in advertising should return multiples to your bottom line. However, often, most business owners when asked what their advertising return on investment (ROI) is, usually just shrug their shoulders. Through proper testing and measuring protocols you will be able to know your ROI, not only for your advertising budget, but also for each advertisement placed.

Advertising could be thought of as a way to purchase customers! As such, if you are making wise purchases, the price that you are paying for each customer, on average, will return to you at least enough profit to cover the cost of the advertisement. Your breakeven point is where return is exactly equal to the amount of your advertising spend, and therefore effectively your advertising budget is zero! And once you understand your advertising ROI and break even, you are ahead of most businesses because you are now able to improve. If you aren't measuring, how can you know if your ROI is increasing or decreasing and whether it makes sense to advertise or not?

Scores of business owners have told me, "Our advertising is too complicated to figure its return." So, here are four simple steps to start measuring advertising ROI:

Tracing Enquiry Origins

First, train your sales staff to ask and record how each enquiry learnt about your business. You could also have unique offers associated with each advertisement for an item or service that has value to the prospect but very low cost to you.

Another approach is to run an integrated marketing campaign with a personalised website which contains a questionnaire designed to drive serious prospects to you. Marketing metrics will be automatically captured.

Measuring Conversion

The next step is to measure how many enquiries are converted into sales – your conversion rate. Some advertisements might produce more enquiries than another, but provide fewer conversions to a sale because of the type of prospects the advertisement attracts!

Lifelong Value of Your Customers

The last metric needed is the average lifelong value of your customers. You need to decide whether once you get a customer, you are likely to continue getting repeat business or if you need to advertise again to get repeat purchases. Most businesses fit the former scenario and can, through good service, have customers coming back to them again and again.

Calculate Your Advertising ROI

With this data, the ROI calculation is simple. Multiply the average lifetime sale value by your profit margin. Multiply that by the number of enquiries generated by the advertising campaign, times your conversion rate for that campaign, and you have your profit produced by that campaign. Divide that by your investment into that campaign and you have your ROI. Mathematically it looks like this:

Enquiries x Conversion x Lifetime Value x Profit Margin
Investment

Gathering some of the data required for the ROI calculation was once a daunting task. However, with the profusion of internet-based marketing and CRM systems specifically designed for acquiring and reporting customer acquisition information, this is now possible for every business.

Once you understand where you are spending and what return you are getting through each avenue, you can begin to make changes to your campaigns to make sure that you consistently improve your ROI.

How to Qualify in a 10-Minute Call

"The cost of being wrong is less than the cost of doing nothing."

Seth Godin

Research indicates that in general around 80% of marketing leads never convert into sales. That's a huge number of leads that you must filter through. You don't want to be wasting valuable time and energy on this 80%, you need to figure out if your lead is one of the 20% that will convert, and you need to do that fast.

As most good salespeople understand, what kills your business is never the prospect who says no but the prospect who says maybe. And most of the above 80% will never really say no, thereby increasing the size of your pipeline and your workload, while never really leading to bottom line impact.

However, at the same time, you need to earn your prospect's trust. If you qualify them, but they don't trust you, they're not going to want to buy from you.

Here is a systematic approach to qualifying leads and earning their trust at the same time – in just a 10-minute call.

Minute 1: Start strong, and position yourself correctly.

There's no time for long-winded rapport questions. This is a qualifying call – you want to get into the deep part fast. But you don't want to completely eradicate an introduction so it's important that you set the stage correctly.

And you want to set it up such that the prospect is on the stage, not you. Most salespeople want to do a song and dance to impress the prospect so that they'll buy.

It's much more powerful to position yourself as the one making the decision – you're trying to qualify them, not convince them to buy from you.

An example you can use: 'What we're going to do on this call is find out a little more about you and find out if or how I can help you. If not, I'll be the first to tell you that and I will help point you in the right direction. If I can, then we'll talk about the next steps. We're going to move quickly, so this won't take a lot of your time. Is that OK?'

Minute 2: How and why did they come to you?

What you want to delve into first is how they found out about you, and why they're approaching you at this stage. This gives you context for how to approach them.

Context is important. If they've come to you as a referral, you know they've had a bit of priming. If they've seen a fleeting Facebook ad from you, you know that they may not know a whole lot about what you do yet.

An example you can use: 'Can I quickly ask, where did you hear about us? And why have you decided to approach us at this point?'

Minute 3: Get an overview of your prospect.

This one depends on who your audience is, but the basic idea is that you want to get a top-level summary of what they do and who they are. The idea here is to find out if they match your target niche.

The danger at this point is that your prospect could end up rambling on about themselves for a long time. The way to mitigate that is to give them a time limit, and ask them two questions, not just one. When you ask two questions, your prospect is likely to want to finish their answers quicker.

An example you can use (for B2B): 'In 30 seconds, tell me what it is your business does. Who do you help, and what is the problem that you solve?'

Minute 4: Find out the bridge they want to cross.

Here you want to figure out exactly where your prospect is right now, and where it is they eventually want to be.

What this also does is bring to the front of their mind their ultimate goals, and puts you in a perfect position to explain the bridge that can get them there. You will do this towards the end of the call.

An example you can use (again, for B2B): 'As a bit of a personal question, can I just ask you what was your [key metric] figure for last month? What do you want that to be eventually?'

Minute 5: Identify what's in the way.

Now that you've shown them that they're not where they want to be, you need to help them clarify exactly why it is they're unable to get there. Here you're trying to understand the issues preventing them from getting to their goal.

The beauty of this is that you're asking them about it, rather than trying to guess. By pulling this information out of them, you're not only learning about their very specific problems, but you're also able to immediately position yourself as the solution to this problem – so they will then credit you with taking them across the bridge that you just showed them they want to cross.

An example you can use: 'So what do you think is missing right now?'

Minute 6: Figure out what they hope to get from you.

If you've got this far, then your prospect will have some sort of expectations of you. You must know what they're expecting to get out of you before you can decide if you can help them.

If they're expecting you to walk on water, then they're probably not going to qualify. However, if they're expecting something you are likely able to offer, that will make it very easy to pitch to them at the end of the call.

An example you can use: 'So how were you hoping I would be able to help you today?'

Minute 7: Find out the immediacy.

Sometimes you're going to have prospects that will need your services – but only once they go through steps A, B and C first. Or what you're offering is useful to them, but it's just not important right now.

If the problem isn't immediate, it's going to be a tough sell and they probably aren't going to buy. A qualified lead is someone who needs what you have on offer as a priority.

An example you can use: 'Is this a later thing for you, or a more immediate need?' (Note: you want to start with mentioning 'later' – it will ensure that you pull out those who really find it an immediate thing and aren't just going with it because you suggested it was an immediate thing.)

Minute 8-9: Restate their problems back to them.

Now's the time for you to earn their trust and respect. If you've been listening carefully to them and taking notes, you should now be able to feed back to them exactly what it is they desire, and what it is that's preventing them from getting there.

If you can articulate their problems and desires better than they can, they'll immediately associate the solution with you.

An example you can use: 'Based on everything you have told me, I think I can say that you ultimately want [the things they want]. However, it seems like [the problems] are what's holding you back. Does that seem fair?'

Minute 10: Close the deal, or close the door.

The last minute is for you to close off the conversation. By now you should have a clear idea of whether they are qualified or not.

If they're qualified, you'll want to explain to them what the next step is in your sales funnel.

If you've realised that they're not right for you, then you politely let them know that they are not a good fit. If you know another business or person that might be able to help them, refer them onwards – you'll earn a lot of goodwill from that.

An example you can use (qualified): 'I said at the start that I was going to figure out if I could help you or not. I have some good news: your issues are exactly what I'm equipped to deal with. Our next step is [your next step, another call maybe or a face to face meeting] and there you will be able to [the benefits of that next step, such as be able to figure out the best solution from our selection of products for XXX problem].'

And another example you can use (non-qualified): 'I said at the start that I was going to figure out if I could help you or not. Unfortunately, I don't think we're quite the right fit because of [your reasons]. However, I know of [friend/another business] who is much more likely to be able to help you, do you want me to tell them about you?'

And there you have it: in just 10 minutes you've quickly established whether your lead is likely to eventually convert (and primed them for that) or not.

Six Marketing Lessons From Santa Claus

"Imagination is more important than knowledge. For knowledge is limited to all we now know and understand, while imagination embraces the entire world, and all there ever will be to know and understand."

Albert Einstein

They say one of the best ways of learning is to mimic the best. People in the UK spend on average £225 at Christmas – PLUS £343 on gifts! And considering the number of people in the country that celebrate Christmas, that's some hefty spending that Santa's managed to rack up.

And he gets all the perks of milk and mince pies laid out for him in every house. So how does he do it? Let's see what marketing lessons we can take from one of the most popular figures in the world – Santa Claus!

Lesson 1: Keep Your Promises

Santa Claus is Coming to Town

You run down the stairs on Christmas morning and the presents… aren't there. First, you're confused. Then you're angry. Then you're disappointed. Promises of gifts were made, but then were not followed through. You start to dislike Santa. You don't trust Santa anymore. You don't love Santa anymore.

Santa doesn't make this mistake and nor should you; if you don't deliver as promised, your marketing isn't going to help you. In fact, it's going to hurt you and your reputation quite significantly if your marketing messages are incongruent with your delivery. So, make sure you've got a secure delivery system in place.

Lesson 2: Always Be Giving

A Bag Full of Toys

Santa is widely loved by people because he's always handing out gifts to people. People love him because he gives them things. It is that simple.

Think about how your marketing messages sound. Do you sound like you're trying to 'get' something from your customers?

Bring the value that you're providing your customers upfront and centre of your marketing message. Deliver value year-round and you'll earn loyal customers that come back to you repeatedly.

Lesson 3: Build Your List – and Qualify It!

He's Making a List, Checking it Twice

Santa doesn't just make a list. He checks it twice. He even finds out who's been naughty and nice!

Santa has been gathering information and consistently building his list for years. More importantly, he has also been consistently qualifying it. It's important to ask – who of your customers or clients are suitable for your business?

Who are the nice ones that deserve your best gifts?

Lesson 4: Be Recognisable

A Belly Like a Bowl Full of Jelly

Santa has arguably one of the most recognised uniforms in the world. That big red suit with the white trimming sets hearts alight immediately.

What is it about your company's branding that makes it instantly recognisable?

You need to have something – a uniform, a logo, even a colour – that you can claim as your own and that people will immediately recognise as yours. Why? Then you can be constantly visible without even being there.

Santa is present in almost every shopping centre in the world – but he's not actually there, is he?

Lesson 5: Systemise

Elves, Reindeer, Malls and Parents

Santa doesn't do most of the work. About four days of the year he's on top of it, but for the rest of it he's relaxing. How? He has representatives in every shopping mall drumming up the crowds. He even has the mums and dads delivering gifts for him and the elves making and packing. He has clear systems in place that run without his direct input.

Make it your mission to systemise at least parts of your business. Hire a hardworking team to make you look good (your elves), create a great delivery process (your reindeer), run repeatable self-promotion events (mall representatives), and create autonomous groups that can manage things locally (the parents).

Lesson 6: Limit Your Access

I'm Sending a Letter to Santa Claus

You can't call 1800-SANTA to get a direct line to Santa Claus. He's far too important to be that accessible. If you want to get a message to Santa, you're going to have to put in a bit of effort, get out a pen and paper and write to him. Even then, the elves will screen the letter and if they can deal with it in the factory, Santa never needs to be bothered. He can stay in his cottage, chilling out with a few icy cocktails with Mrs Claus.

Only the most important of messages get through to bother him.

Are you making yourself too accessible to your customers/clients? As the business owner, your time should be incredibly valuable and precious. If you're readily accessible, then your customers or clients may start to think you're not that busy, or worse, not that successful.

Customer service is critical, of course. Set up a system for it – there should be someone else answering the phone, screening calls and bringing you only the most important things to deal with personally.

The man in the big red suit has a bit of a head start, but it isn't that hard to grow big fast. Just learn from the best, implement the right tools and strategies and you could be relaxing in your own North Pole before long, while your elves get the work done without you.

The Unlimited Marketing Budget

"It's not the resources but resourcefulness that ultimately makes the difference."

Tony Robbins

Business owners often have three flawed mindsets that keep them from successful marketing:

1. Marketing is a big cost.
2. We should market to as many people as we possibly can.
3. We should 'get our name out there'.

You may look at those and say, 'Of course – because they're true.' Unfortunately, these beliefs often guide your marketing in the wrong direction.

Instead, follow these seven steps, and you'll find yourself churning out marketing that not only generates a high return on investment but also generates consistent quality leads.

Step 1: Define Measurable Marketing Objectives (MMOs)

Measurable is the key word here – move away from vague objectives like 'grow more' or 'get more leads'. Put a number to it. Get as specific as you possibly can about the who, where, what and how.

An example for a flooring installation business might be:

'Generate 75 qualified leads from interior designers in Q2 for core flooring installation services.'

You may ask, how do you determine that number? Well the best place to start is to look at your Measurable Business Objectives (MBOs) – what do you want your business to achieve (be specific!)?

Then ensure that your MMOs align with your MBOs.

Step 2: Tightly Define Your 'Who'

The target market is important. You know this. But are you getting as specific as you should be?

In the example from the previous point, you may think that they've got their target market clear: interior designers. I would call that a loose target.

When you think of your marketing, don't think of it as marketing to a crowd of people. Think of it more like communicating to an individual – just doing it many, many times.

To create that unlimited marketing budget, you need to understand not your target *market* but your target *person*. That is, who is the ideal person for you to sell your product to? What does this person like? What are the common problems this person faces? How does this person communicate?

If you can't immediately think of who that person is, here are a few rules of thumb:

1. He/she should be a raving fan of your business solution.

2. He/she should be easy to reach.

3. He/she should provide a high average value to you.

4. He/she should be likely to provide repeat business.

5. He/she should have an effective lead time.

A good place to start is to choose one of your current or previous clients or customers that was perfect. Start by writing down whatever you know about them, and build around that.

That would just be a beginning. Another way to build a good ideal person is to interview someone that represents your ideal target person – then you get real facts rather than making up things that simply may not be true.

Step 3: Define How You'll Communicate with Them

You need to walk in your ideal target person's shoes and figure out what makes that person tick. This is vital to your marketing because without knowing this, he/she simply won't respond to you.

You need to be able to know what their problem is, and then express that problem better than they can. If you can do that, then you have already won them.

The above mapping of needs and motivations gives you a way to think about your customer's needs.

1. Immediate Needs and Away from Motivation – These are the 'Frustrations' i.e. the things happening right now that your prospect wants to stop.

2. Immediate Needs and Towards Motivation – These are the 'Wants' i.e. the things that the prospect would like to have happening right now.

3. Imagined Needs and Away from Motivation – These are the 'Fears', something the prospect is afraid that if these are not met, they will be dissatisfied.

4. Imagined Needs and Towards Motivation – These are the 'Aspirations', something the prospect wishes for in the future.

Make sure you have outlined at least three Needs in each quadrant to be able to individually consider the different issues in each quadrant and how your business will solve them.

Step 4: Work Out the Acquisition Costs

When creating a marketing budget, you must first think about the *allowable budget to acquire a client*. This is something that most business owners often ignore.

The question you are trying to answer is how much you can spend in marketing to get a client or customer. You do this by simply pegging it to the gross profit per product.

In the flooring example, if the average order value is £800, and the gross margin (the percentage of sales that is gross profit) is 30% of that, then there's £240 that can be spent on marketing strategies to acquire one interior designer – that is their *allowable acquisition cost*.

You could also go a step further and figure out the *lifetime value* of an acquired customer.

Again, in the above example, if the ideal interior designer buys twice from them every year and typically for five years, the allowable acquisition cost goes up to £2,400 (£240 x 2 x 5).

Step 5: Choose your Channel, Offer and Cost

If you aren't a big business yet, then your primary focus needs to be on brand activation, rather than awareness.

This means that every piece of marketing you do should have a clear call to action (CTA) with a strong reason. The best and most effective way of achieving this is to bundle an offer with the CTA.

Coca-Cola's 'Happiness' campaigns are a good example of awareness campaigns: they are simply brand building. They dominate enough market share to not require strong, convincing reasons to encourage people to take action.

In a cluttered market, however, your prospects need to have a strong reason why they should get in touch with you, rather that someone else in your sector.

An example can be something as simple as 'Get a £200 voucher towards your next order when you call us at XXX'.

You then need to decide how much you're spending and what channel you're using. Don't take a stab in the dark – measure this carefully.

Here is an example. Let's say you have two options: 1) Newspaper adverts that cost £1,200 per insert and 2) Flyers that cost £400 for 1,000 flyers (including delivery).

Now let's say that the readership of the newspaper is 2,000 and the typical conversion rate for it from readership to enquiry is 1%. And let's say the conversion rate of the flyers is also 1%.

You then would expect to get 20 enquiries from newspaper adverts and 10 enquiries from flyers.

Is this enough to tell you which channel is best? Let's dig a little deeper with the earlier interior designer example.

Average Value of order:	£800
Gross Margin:	30% (£240)
Annual Number of Transactions:	10 (2 every year for 5 years)
Total gross profit per customer:	£2,400
Conversion rate from enquiry to sales:	10%

With these numbers, you can then do some calculations on how much profit you're going to get from each channel:

Newspaper Advert

Total Customers Acquired: 2 (10% of 20 enquiries)

Total Profit: £2,400 x 2 = £4,800

Net Position: £4,800 - £1,200 = £3,600

Return on Investment:	£3,600 ÷ £1,200 = 3 times

Flyers

Total Customers Acquired:	1 (10% of 10 enquiries)
Total Profit:	£2,400
Net Position:	£2,400 - £400 = £2,000
Return on Investment:	£2,000 ÷ £400 = 5 times

So actually, both strategies are great but simply directing all your marketing budget to flyers could result in a massive increase in your profitability.

Step 6: Measure the Return on Your Marketing Investment

Once you've chosen your channel and run a campaign you then need to measure the return from your marketing investment. You need to figure out what the actual numbers are.

Use the same calculations as above, but with your actual numbers rather than predicted ones and figure out what your conversion rates are.

Importantly, find out your final net position and return. If you identify one channel that systematically makes you more return than what you invest, you've just found the secret to having an unlimited marketing budget.

Step 7: Automate Your Unlimited Budget Spend

When you have found a strategy that works, it's time to systemise it.

You should explore automation tools to see if there are automated systems that can help systemise the approach. Then train your team so they can maintain the process with minimal input from you.

Then begin looking for the next strategy to generate another source of unlimited marketing budget.

Top 20 Killer Sales Questions

"One of the best predictors of ultimate success ... isn't natural talent or even industry expertise, but how you explain your failures and rejections."

Daniel H Pink

Making a sale is very much an art – the art of education and persuasion. Like a lot of art forms, there are those with a natural flair for it who can do it without even thinking. However, boosting your sales by becoming better at persuasion is an art that can be taught, can be learnt, and can be mastered.

This set of 20 questions, inspired by Philip Hesketh, author of *How to Persuade and Influence People*, is a collection to keep in your arsenal for whenever you need to get that little bit more information to understand your prospect better and help them make the right choice.

Print them out, memorise them, and when you get stuck in a sales conversation, pull one of them out.

1. What is the most frustrating thing for you about...?

2. What makes you say that? (Why do you say that?/Can you give me some background on that?/What draws you to that conclusion?)

3. What do you see as the purpose of this meeting exactly?

4. What do you think causes...? (Do you have a perspective on that?)

5. What have you done so far to address the problem?

6. What would you do differently if...?

7. What is likely to happen if...?

8. What won't happen if...?

9. What are the implications for you if...?

10. Who benefits most from...?

11. What would you like in the future?/
    In an ideal world, what would you have?
    What would success look like for you?/
    What would make this perfect for you?

12. Is anyone else involved in the buying decision?

13. What are the key drivers for the other people involved?

14. Have you spoken to anyone else about this?

15. What is the most pressing issue you are facing in the business right now?

16. What would be easiest for you?

17. How important is that to you?

18. Will that be enough for you?

19. I agree you should think about it. Often when our clients say that it's because there is an issue they need to address. Is that the case with you?

20. What would we have to do to make you go ahead with this?

A key quality you will note in a lot of the above questions is that they are all open-ended questions – they make the customer think and help you dig deeper.

Primal Price Fear

"If you really want to do something, you'll find a way. If you
don't, you'll find an excuse."

Jim Rohn

One of the most successful strategies to increase profitability
is a very simple one: increase your prices.

Simple, but not easy. Most of us are afraid of increasing our
price because we fear being out-competed by our competitors
who keep dropping their prices just to get a sale. The critical
difference here is that a competitor who does that is selling
on Price as against selling on Value. Value here is what you
create for your customers with your products and services
and the value that you generate for your own company – your
bottom line.

And increasing prices is possible not just when the tide is
up but also when the economic scenario is looking bleak –
if you deliver value against what you charge. Will you lose
customers with the increase in price? You probably will lose
some, but remember that the profit you make is a lot more
important than the number of customers you have. If your
overall profitability increases, losing a few customers may not
be a bad thing at all.

Here are a few easy steps to increase your price with few or
no complaints:

1. Against each of your products and services, mark what you sold them for in this month last year.

2. Sort this list so you have the highest value items on the top of the list.

3. Remove from this list the products and services which you believe are the most price sensitive.

4. For the top 10% of items in this list, increase your price by at least 10%.

5. Test and measure results.

6. Repeat with the next 10% of the items in the list.

In general, if you are at a 30% gross margin and implement a 10% increase, you can afford to lose up to a quarter of your current sales volume with your gross profit still increasing!

Creating Snappy Offers

"I am all for conversations, but you need to have a message."

Renee Blodgett

In inbound marketing, a lead magnet is something which makes people engage with you for the first time. Remember, not *transact* with you but *engage* with you because you are offering something of value to them but typically not charging them for it. This is your way to build a list of people who are interested in your products and services so you can sharpen your marketing approach towards them.

The first principle of building a lead magnet is that you need to keep your avatar or your target person in your mind and design specifically for this person. Once you have done this, you need to think of what combination of perceived risk and perceived value you want your lead magnet to have for the customer.

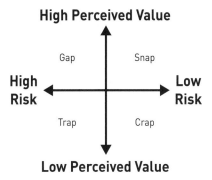

The above model, inspired by Taki Moore, Online Lead Generation Expert, maps Risk and Value to break the variety of offers you can make into four broad quadrants.

The Crap Quadrant

In this quadrant, the risk is low for the target person but at the same time perceived value is also very low. There are a surprising number of businesses who make an offer in this quadrant – an offer to sign up for a newsletter is often exactly here. This is not a lead magnet which will attract your target customer simply because the perceived value is very low. It may in fact attract people who are never going to be customers.

The Trap Quadrant

In this quadrant, the risk is high and the perceived value is low. Often, the perceived risk may simply be the risk of losing an hour of their time or effort they must make. Offers for meeting over coffee may fall into this category as would offers to attend one-day sell-fests. This typically does not position you as a high-value business.

The Gap Quadrant

In this quadrant, the risk is high, but desire is high as well. This is where the customer clearly sees the value of what is on offer but believes the risk – of either time or effort or losing face or being hard sold to – to be very high. This may be an offer for a financial review or a property inspection or even a knowledge-based video which is too long and therefore not desired enough in this world of instant gratification. This is usually a good lead magnet but often works better with people who are already engaged with your business in some way or another and not cold prospects. There is a gap here that can be resolved.

The Snap Quadrant

In this quadrant, there is high perceived value and low risk and therefore prospects would love to 'snap' up the lead magnet that you are offering. The risk is lower because often you only ask them for an email address and sometimes not even that (considering you can Google them) and offer a tool or one page 'how to' document which has high perceived value.

Once you have initiated some form of engagement with a completely cold prospect, you can now begin to really sharpen your marketing towards the specific value that they have perceived.

Price and Value

"Customer's perception is your reality."

Kate Zabriskie

I was at a toyshop with my son and he was looking at a few toys. He picked up one he liked and said, "Mumma, I want to buy this one." I looked at what he had picked up. It was a £5 toy and made of some clearly cheap material. I said, "That looks good but I'm not sure I would want to spend money on it. Let's look a bit more before we decide." We kept looking and he soon found something else that he liked, this time a £15 toy. I looked at the toy and said, "Let's go for it. This looks interesting."

As we finished our shopping and left the store, my son was looking a little puzzled. He looked at me and said, "You said no for a toy which was £5 and you actually ended up spending three times more. Why's that? I thought you'd agree for that £5 toy."

I explained, "As a buyer, when we were at the shop, we did not really have a budget in mind for how much we wanted to spend. I was therefore looking for value and not price. Really, even if I had a budget of £5, I would still try to get as much value in that budget as I could."

Here's a simple way to define value:

Value = Benefits – Cost

The cost or price of the product could be really anything, but if the benefit or the perceived benefit to the buyer is higher, the price really does not matter.

As a business owner, you should always be focused on increasing the value to your customers.

The relatively easier way of doing this is to simply reduce the price – that's your discounting or low-cost strategies. Unfortunately, discounting is a bottomless pit and is often the bane of many a business.

The other, better way is to increase the benefits or the perception of benefit to the customer. Very simply, the benefit is the problem that's getting solved by using your product or service, or an improvement to the customer's current situation.

What you need to think, as a business owner, is: How do I increase the benefits for my customers and communicate it loud and clear so they know that these are the benefits that they're getting?

In fact, you should be charging the right *price* for the *value* that you're extending. Do not discount your services or products. Despite what they may tell you, your customer is keen on value and not on price.

The price that you charge may have some relevance to the material cost, the time and effort that goes into extending that service and product, but that's not the only thing. What you need to keep in mind is the extent of benefit that you're providing to your customer. What it means in terms of emotional value, in terms of material value that they are getting out of your services and products.

Lead your marketing and all your selling with value first. Once you can demonstrate the value that your product or service will convey to the customer, the price discussion is going to be a lot more straightforward.

Part V:
Management

With the greatest leader above them,

people barely know one exists.

Next comes one whom they love and praise.

Next comes one who they fear.

Next comes one whom they despise and defy.

When a leader trusts no one,

no one trusts him.

The great leader speaks little.

He never speaks carelessly.

He works without self-interest and leaves no trace.

When all is finished, the people say, "We did it all by ourselves."

Tao Te Ching

Say Do Co

"Be the change you wish to see in the world."

Mahatma Gandhi

A young boy had become obsessed with eating a lot of sugar. His mother was very upset but no matter how much she scolded him, she could not rid him of the habit. She finally decided to take her son to see Mahatma Gandhi, the boy's idol.

She had to walk many miles across the country, for hours under scorching sun, to finally reach Gandhi's ashram. There, she recounted her difficult journey and shared with Gandhi her unpleasant situation:

"Bapu, my son eats too much sugar. It is not good for his health. I know that he respects you so much that he will stop if you ask him to. Would you please advise him to stop eating it?"

Gandhi listened to the woman carefully, thought for a while and replied, "Please come back after two weeks. I will talk to your son."

Surprised, the woman agreed and took the boy by the hand and went home. She made the long journey home and two weeks later made it once again as Gandhi had requested.

When they arrived, Gandhi looked directly at the boy and said, "Son, you should stop eating sugar. It is not good for your health."

The boy nodded and promised he would not continue this habit any longer.

The puzzled mother turned to Gandhi and asked, "Bapu, why didn't you just tell him that two weeks ago, when I brought him here to see you the first time?"

Gandhi smiled and said, "Two weeks ago, I had no right to tell him to give up sugar as I had not given up sugar myself and did not know how it would feel."

Most people expect a lot more of other people and too little of themselves. If you expect a high level of integrity from people around you, the first step is to start expecting a high level of integrity from yourself. Here's a simple rule leadership coach Marshall Goldsmith teaches to make this concept a real, practical concept for your team and for yourself: say what you are going to do; do what you said you will be doing; and communicate as you are doing it, when you finish doing it or when you get stuck trying to do it.

Now, in business context, integrity is simply expecting each person in the team (including yourself) to commit to action that is required and then take the action that each person has committed to. However, it should not stop there and the problem is that unfortunately there will always be curve balls thrown at you in business which may mean that you are not able to do what you said in a timely manner. For everyone around you, when this happens and if you've not kept everyone informed well in advance, it will always come as a bad surprise and impact upon your own trustworthiness.

The third element of integrity for business is therefore communication – everyone in the team needs to know that if they get stuck on any commitment of theirs, they need to communicate with the rest of the team. Importantly, they also need to communicate if they are not stuck with a basic progress report. This is how everyone else in the team, particularly the business owner, can be on top of the situation and potentially provide the support or guidance to the team member who might be struggling to do what he/she has committed.

The point of working in a business towards the same objective is to not have to fight your own corner but to have a team of other people who have each other's back. This is what leads to true long-term progress for the business; you may move faster if you go alone but you will go a lot further if you go along with your team.

Camels and Elephants

"Those who cannot change their minds cannot change anything."

George Bernard Shaw

A long time ago in central Africa, there was a trader who decided to travel with his wares from the north to the south, across desert and jungle, to a place he had heard would fetch astounding value for his wares.

The first half of the journey was dangerous jungle country. He sought out the best advice he could find and decided that the best way to undertake this journey would be to carry his wares on a herd of elephants. Elephants, of course, are incredibly strong animals able to travel long distances and, more importantly, most carnivores give them a wide berth.

As he travelled through the jungle, he also marvelled at the adaptability of these animals – they could swim across rivers, find their own food as they travelled and seemed to understand what he wanted them to do. He grew attached to them, gave them individual 'pet' names and through many an adventure finally reached the other end of the jungle.

For the second leg of his journey now, he had arid desert ahead of him. As he rested at the edge of the desert, he was approached by multiple people trying to sell him camels. Now, as a practice, he hated hard-selling techniques. The more people tried to convince him that he should trade his elephants for camels, the more he dug his heels in and resisted. These animals (the elephants) had helped him through an incredible journey over the last few months. He had shared many adventures with them. How could he now leave them when the environment had changed? Did he not have a duty to take care of them? Was he not responsible for teaching them how they could become good camels? Besides, they did have flat feet like camels to help them stay up on sand, small eyes to help prevent sand blowing into their eyes and hard skin to take the rigours of the desert.

So, he started off on the second leg of his journey with his herd of elephants. He soon started noticing things that he had not picked up before. First, his journey was slower because the elephants kept sinking into the sand. He realised that they are quite heavy animals, weighing about 10 times more than a camel. He also realised that they need to keep eating and drinking – and there is no food and water for miles in a desert.

By the time he reached the first oasis, half his herd had died.

He traded the rest for camels.

Here's the moral of the story for the businessman: to cross a desert, you need camels, not modified and trained elephants. Often to define the next level for your business, you will need to move away from the current people in your business and hire a completely fresh group. Daunting as this may seem, not only is this the best for your business, it probably is, in the long run, the best for your employees.

When you rethink your business goals and where you see your business three to five years from now, first define clearly the kind of people you need to get there. And then decide whether the people you have currently can be trained and challenged to get you there. Don't decide your business goals based on what your current team and resources can achieve. What got you *here* may not be sufficient to get you *there*!

Flying in Formation

"The team played very well and I was delighted to help
out with three goals."

Ronaldinho

Most people know that geese always seem to fly in the V formation. As each bird flaps its wings, it creates an uplift for the bird immediately behind it. By flying in this V formation, the whole flock adds a significant amount (up to 70% according to some research) of greater flying range than if an individual bird was flying on its own.

Sharing a common direction and a sense of community gets geese wherever they are going more quickly and easily because they are travelling on the thrust of one another. When a goose falls out of formation, it suddenly feels the drag and resistance of trying to go it alone – and quickly tries to get back into formation to take advantage of the lifting power of the bird in front.

What can we as business teams learn from the geese? How much easier does life and business become if we stay in formation and aligned with other people who are headed the same way we are? How often do we check with our teams that we are indeed flying in formation?

Interestingly also, when the head goose gets tired, it moves back in the formation and another goose flies point. It is sensible to take turns doing demanding jobs, whether with people or with geese flying south. A leader's job is tough. But a leader's job is not always to be at the front – sometimes leadership happens from within the team.

Finally, and this is important, when a goose gets sick or is wounded by gunshot, and falls out of formation, two other geese fall out with that goose and follow it down to lend help and protection. They stay with the fallen goose until it can fly or until it dies and only then do they launch out on their own, or with another formation to catch up with their group. This is what teamwork is about.

You don't always have to look far and wide to understand the secrets of great and winning teams. Sometimes you just have to look up!

Delegation vs Abdication

"Management by objectives works if you first think through your objectives. Ninety percent of the time you haven't."

Peter Drucker

Too often I meet business owners who are pulling their hair out due to the lack of performance and dedication of their employees. When asked what their biggest business frustration is, they generally reply "finding good people!"

When we peel back the layers, we find that the cause of the problem is more often than not an employer who is either hands on or hands off and never really focused on handing over. And when they do decide to be hands off, too many tasks are abdicated and not delegated.

The difference? When an employer abdicates a task or role, he is abandoning all responsibility. A task is simply handed over to employees and they are expected to perform because 'they should know what to do'!

The result: the employee struggles, things go bottom up and the employer must step in to fix the problems. After a while the employer, out of sheer frustration at the number of problems arising, takes over that role again crying, 'I tried giving them the job but if I want it done properly I must do it myself.'

The employee on the other hand is now confused because he thought he was doing a good job. Sick of being yelled at by the boss, employees become reluctant to take basic decisions.

There are, however, solutions. The first key to a winning team is strong leadership – and strong leaders delegate, they do not abdicate!

Delegation relies on the owner keeping control of the situation, but not the work. The task is explained, training provided, performance measurements set and the responsibility (with consequences and rewards) assigned.

Will the employee still make mistakes? Of course they will! But they are not left to flounder from mistake to mistake. They are supervised, and with the business owner's input taken through the steps of the process until a solution is found. And at this stage, the employee with the responsibility fixes the problem.

Over time, employees develop a clear sense of what is required, as well as understanding the importance of the task. They develop the confidence to really perform in their role, and know that if they make a mistake, they must fix it.

Because strong leaders keep measuring performance and have regular performance reviews with their team, each employee knows clearly that their future advancement within the company depends upon their own performance.

The business owners, on the other hand, can now trust their employees. There are fewer frustrations, more consistent results and less workload on the boss. Everyone is now working together as a team and not as individuals.

Now you have a winning team!

Batman and Robin

"Management is doing things right; Leadership is
about doing the right things."

Peter Drucker

Who's the Robin to your Batman in your business?

As the idiom goes, 'No man is an island'. In any big business in the world, the person that visibly leads the company is almost always backed up by an equally powerful and motivated second in command – the 'right-hand man' or the 'wingman' or whatever you want to call them.

We're talking about the Steve Wozniak to Steve Jobs, the Paul Allen to Bill Gates, the Robin to Batman, the yin to the yang.

Choosing this person in your business – if you haven't already chosen them – is a big step and one that deserves some very serious consideration. This person will likely play a large part in whether your business grows to new levels of success, or falters and plateaus.

Here are three simple rules of thumb that you can use to help guide your decision in hiring and nurturing your second in command to help grow your business.

1. Look Within

The first place to look for Robin is often within the business.

Having someone who has experience in your organisation and knows how it works is an invaluable asset that usually cannot be found in an external candidate.

Hiring someone internally also breeds loyalty within your organisation, and while there are several factors that help build a loyal team, this is often one of the hardest traits to maintain in employees. Witnessing a colleague ascend the career path within the organisation indicates there is room to grow and climb in your organisation and they are not stuck in a 'dead end' job.

2. Ambition is Key

There will always be people in your organisation who are afraid of the ambition of their own team members. They see it as a threat to their position in the organisation. The key giveaway to this behaviour is when they consistently ignore or even diminish the superstars in their team. There seems to be a fear that if someone has a lot of ambition, they will seek to take over. If the person with this personality trait is the business leader himself/herself, he/she will very likely surround himself/herself with incapable 'yes' men and women.

Ambition is the key to driving a thriving business. It is often even more important than talent when it comes to getting good results. Think about it: ambition is what drove you to where you are now, and where your business is now. Ambition is energy and motivation to achieve success.

Identify someone who is willing and able to focus their energy into your business to help it grow and nurture them by letting them take decisions and risks where they know you will have their back – even if they make mistakes. And you will find yourself with the kind of person who takes initiative and goes beyond what *needs* to be done and instead looks towards what *should* be done.

3. The Lightning Strike Test

Here is the million-pound question: Does the person you are thinking of pass the 'Lightning Strike' test? That is, if you were to be struck by lightning and were bedridden for a couple of months, would you be able to rest knowing that this person was in charge?

It is as simple as a yes or no, and it all comes down to trust – in the systems you have set up for your business and the people you have in the business who will follow the systems and can be trusted to handle any exceptions the way you would want them handled. A business that can run without you is one which is truly 'successful'.

If you have found someone who could handle your business for a few months without your attention, then you may have just found your pathway to the next level of success for your business.

Choosing this person is no simple choice for any business owner or decision maker in a business. The growth of your business massively depends on this person's skills and how well they fit into your company. However, if you are looking to set your business on to the path of growth, and take it to where you are no longer required to play a constantly active part in it, then this is one of the most important decisions that you absolutely must make.

And you might just smile when you hear,

'Holy Profitability, Batman' on the next holiday you take.

Three Gold Stars

"Surround yourself with the best people you can find,
delegate authority, and don't interfere as long as the policy
you've decided upon is being carried out."

Ronald Reagan

Most business owners realise that it is critical for their team to have Key Performance Indicators to allow for measurable performance reporting and understanding how each person is doing against what they should be doing.

What some forget, however, is that goals and KPIs should always flow from the top to the bottom, which means you need to be quite clear of your KPIs too as a business owner.

There are three core performance indicators against which every leader should measure themselves.

Common Goal

Your first indicator of performance is that the company has a common goal and that everyone in the business is aligned to that common goal. This may sound simple but I've seen enough business owners being surprised at the variety of answers they receive when they ask their team what their goal is.

If you have a written down common goal which you have communicated and explained to your team in the last quarter, give yourself a gold star.

Right Team

Your second indicator of performance is whether you have the right people in your team to help you achieve your common goal. If you had to fire everyone in your business and start all over again, how many of them would you rehire? Would you rehire yourself? Are all the roles within the organisation being filled by the right person who is accountable and responsible? Or do you have some dire recruitment needs either because important activities are not being done or because work is flowing to where it gets done and a few people are overextended?

Remember one of your key roles is hiring and managing talent. Would you give yourself a gold star here? What needs to change in the next quarter for you to truly deserve a gold star?

Right Activities

The third indicator of performance is to make sure that the right people are doing the right activities which will help the company move towards that one common goal.

Do you have systems in place to ensure that each team member is working on the right activities? How often do you review the systems and the activities? Are you tracking both outcomes and activities for each member of your team? Does your team outperforming on their Key Performance Indicators mean that you will automatically have outperformed on business goals?

If you are confident that this is happening, give yourself another gold star.

Look back at your responses to all the above questions and then answer this one. Are you working 'on' the business or 'in' the business?

The Six Hoops Challenge

"I believe in constant recruitment. If I find someone great I
don't wait for an opening to get them onboard."

Shweta Jhajharia

Sales is one of the most difficult areas to work in within a business. This is because it is the most directly measurable: there is no fluff and you are either hitting your targets or you are failing. You are constantly under pressure and constantly facing rejection.

Finding a person for a sales role within your business is therefore not an easy task as the qualities you are looking for may be very different from what you are generally used to looking for in a team member.

Big Ego and High Self-Esteem

While typically socially discouraged, a big ego and proud bearing is an asset in the sales world. A salesperson needs to be able to withstand rejection, and for that they need to be keenly aware and confident of their own skills.

Empathy

To close a sale, the customer needs to be able to relate to what they are buying and who they are buying from. The salesperson needs to understand how the customer *feels* and guide those feelings towards helping them make the correct buying decision. A good salesperson will always ensure that the client wins when they buy the product/service.

Storytelling

Storytelling is one of the most effective forms of persuasion. After a presentation, 63% of attendees remember the stories, while only 5% remember the statistics (Source: Chip & Dan Heath). If your salesperson can tell a good story, it is likely that they will also be good at selling your product.

With these three qualities in mind, let's walk through our suggested interview process to help you hone into the right salesperson for your business.

First Hoop: Find out how they're built

Don't launch immediately into their skills. Start by figuring out where they have come from and how they have got to where they are so you can get an idea of who they are as a person.

Be honest with them and tell them that you're going to start by asking them some questions about who they are and what shapes them, and ask them if they agree that recruiting on fit and attitude and not just capability is a better way to hire. This allows them to understand why you are asking personal questions and gets them explicitly to agree to answer them.

You are not asking any questions that could be misconstrued as discrimination, only trying to understand the person.

The questions and prompts you may want to use to draw out their story are:

- Describe instances in your upbringing that have forged you into the person you are today

- In your life, right now, either personal or career-wise, what are you having the most difficulty with?

- What have you learnt from your parents or guardians?

These sorts of questions are going to give your candidate the opportunity to tell a story, helping you figure out how good a storyteller they are. If they are smart, intelligent and a good salesperson, they will ensure that the stories they tell are centred on their strengths – showing their confidence and positive qualities. The lessons they have learnt will also give insight into their empathy, especially what they have learnt from their parents or guardians.

In this first step alone, you begin to get a sense of whether this candidate is your champion. These questions also put the candidate at ease – they are talking of something they should be quite familiar with.

Second Hoop: Look for accomplishments

The next step of questions is discussions of personal and professional accomplishments. Here you are looking for someone who can very quickly rattle off a list of accomplishments. Not only should they be natural high achievers, they should also have the pride and self-confidence to be able to immediately list their achievements. What they think of as achievements also gives you a sense of what achievement is for them – it may not be the same as the kind of achievement levels you are looking for.

Questions that you may want to ask at this stage are:

- Was there a time in your life when despite everything seemingly against you, you still succeeded and achieved great results?

- Are there any other areas in your life where you have made significant achievements? Any sports or hobbies?

- What are the top four things you're proud of?

Third Hoop: Figure out how they measure up

You know what they've done, but have they learnt skills that they can use in other situations? This again will naturally lead from the previous set of questions.

Questions that you may want to ask at this stage are:

- Who is the best salesperson you've ever met? What differentiates you from them?

- Can you tell me a few authors or educators that you have read or that you follow?

- Who would you consider as one of your mentors?

The first question helps you assess not only their skills, but also their ego. The best answer you can get from that question is 'Me'. Then the second half of it doesn't matter anymore – you have a potential superstar in front of you. And if they answer someone else, the second half will give insight into where they feel their 'room to grow' is.

The next question, about their personal education, is also much more important than it initially seems. It will not only reveal their accomplishments, but also their dedication to their own education. A good salesperson will constantly upskill themselves through reading sales books.

Once a candidate's response to this question was, "My current company does not send me for training." This is a big red flag: if your hire is not committed to their own self-learning, they are not going to learn anything other than what you force them to learn. Not exactly the best person to have in your team.

Fourth Hoop: Test their empathy

The next step is to test how well they react to people, and how others react to them. This is arguably one of the more difficult qualities to get out of a candidate, as they'll usually only be able to express things from their point of view.

Questions that you may want to ask at this stage are:

- What are your best memories?
- If I brought your best friend into this interview, what would they say about you?
- Who in your life is your biggest fan? Why?

With each question, you also give the candidate an opportunity to display their strengths and good qualities. If they are not taking advantage of every opportunity, they are not selling themselves to the best of their ability. If they cannot sell themselves, how are they going to sell for you?

Fifth Hoop: Review their CV and see if they have good judgment

This is the point at which you really review the CV along with them. The key insight you are looking for here is whether the person in front of you has been pulled from one job to another or pushed from one job to another.

Questions that you may want to ask at this stage for every position are:

- Why were you hired for this position?

- What made you leave this job?

- Were you unhappy? What was the issue?

- Did you have any disagreement with your line manager? What happened?

- When I call your line manager to ask for your reference (take the details of the line manager here), what would they say you do well?

- What would they say you could develop on?

You want to understand how they behave at work, and what their reasoning is. In the end, you want to draw something controversial out of them to see how they face situations that may involve conflict and be difficult to handle.

One of my clients asked a candidate about their previous boss and the candidate said that one of his previous bosses was "too picky about the little details that didn't matter." Would this person be able to work with you?

Remember that at every stage you need to let the candidate be open and honest and remain impartial while making your notes. Allow the candidate to fully explain themselves before making any judgments on them.

Sixth Hoop: The ultimate ego test

This is the final step, and the one that will seriously separate out the best of the best. Here's how you play it out:

Once you have finished the other steps and you are sure this candidate is a champion, tell them that they're not a champion.

I think one of the best ways to do this is the way Chet Holmes recommends: "You seem like a nice person, but I only have one opening. I need a real superstar. While I'm sure you would do well in many endeavours, this is a very competitive industry and I doubt your skills and personality will hold up in this position. To be truthful, I don't get the impression that you're really a superstar."

Don't be gentle here. Be polite but firm. However, don't be aggressive and don't act judgmental. Don't be aggressive or judgmental. You should practise saying this in a calm, level and neutral voice. However, also make sure you are telling them that you don't think they're suitable rather than softening it. For example, you don't want to say, 'I'm not really sure about you yet' or 'I'm not really convinced you're a champion'. That's too easy.

You'll be surprised at how many salespeople just cave in and accept this. They've just spent a lot of time selling themselves and the moment you give them an objection – something they will get a lot of in their job – they crumble. Doesn't sound very confident, does it?

Champions stick around. Champions fight back. Champions are so sure of themselves that when faced with a statement like that, they'll challenge you.

The best response you can get from them: 'Why is it that you think that?' This is the ultimate question they can throw back at you because they are proving their salesmanship: when faced with a hesitation, ask a question, find out the problem and then solve the problem.

One candidate I was hiring asked me this very question at this stage of the interview and I told her, "You haven't differentiated yourself, haven't proved you're the best of the best." Sure, that was a bit of guidance for her to tell me more, but she delivered.

She sat there for a good five minutes, not only reiterating a lot of what we had talked about, but took the opportunity to bring up other instances where she had achieved amazing things. Not once did I hear anger, resentment or arrogance in her voice – just confident pride in herself.

After that I knew then I'd found my champion. And if you make sure that the people you are hiring have passed through these hoops, you can be quite confident that you'll find yours too.

More is Less

"Perfectionism is slow death."

Hugh Prather

'I wish I could grow my business without ever hiring anyone.'

Does that sound familiar?

For most businesses, this is usually a symptom of a team not performing at a level which the business owner expects them to – either on results or in the culture and value system around them.

Often, on digging deeper, I find the following vicious cycle at play in the business: the business owner has not communicated clearly and frequently what is expected of each team member – in activities that they are required to do, results they are expected to deliver and culture they are expected to follow. Team members are therefore running off in multiple directions – making mistakes, not performing as expected and creating an unpleasant culture for themselves and everyone else. As more and more issues crop up, there is more time spent reacting and firefighting and even less on proactive communication – partially as the work of firefighting is always ongoing and partially because no one really wants to sit together and face the conflict. This in turn leads to further mistakes and even more negativity in the team. And this continues in a downward spiral.

The best solution to this issue is exactly what the business owner has often been avoiding: more communication through structured team meetings. While 'less is more' often makes sense in a large corporate organisation with many people, in most businesses, where the environment is fast changing and every person is really expected to be flexible enough to juggle multiple things, you need to leverage off the collective intelligence that you have in your business through a regular rhythm of team meetings.

More is Less

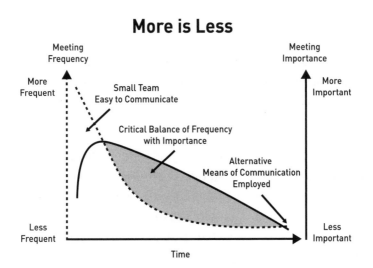

There are several reasons meetings have historically got a bad rap – a significant number of meetings devolve into being completely ineffective and soul crushing. But remember, a meeting is simply a tool – and used incorrectly, most tools are ineffectual. A couple of significant elements often missing from meetings are:

1. Lack of drama (conflict) – heated arguments and demonstrations of passion, as long as they remain constructive, can generate a deeper and broader understanding of the topic.

2. Lack of context – the type of meeting and the organisation of the meeting need to be tailored to the issues being addressed.

Here's a quick checklist to ensure that your meetings are crisp and effective.

1. Define the purpose

What's the purpose of the meeting? Is it to brainstorm, get an update or discuss a problem? Is it to set the activities for the next day/week/quarter or to review the activities of the last day/week/quarter?

Everything stems from the purpose. If you don't know what the end goal is, then your meeting will inevitably lose its shape and clarity.

2. Create an agenda

What's the agenda for the meeting and is everyone attending aware of the agenda in advance? A crisp agenda ensures that everyone comes prepared and you discuss things that are useful to everyone present and everyone can contribute.

3. Set a time limit

Team meetings should not be a long sit down where you are sharing gossip and relaxing. Sure, creating rapport amongst everyone present is important but make sure that your meeting doesn't digress too far from the intended purpose and agenda.

How long do you expect the meeting to take? And five minutes is also a good answer, particularly for daily catch-up meetings.

4. Limit the number of attendees

It is often tempting to have a meeting with the whole company to get that sense of 'togetherness'. Unfortunately, that is often not the best thing for your company. If you want meetings that are going to move your company forward, you need to have the right people attending. If someone does not need to be in the meeting, don't include them.

Every meeting is different and will have unique requirements, so you do need to be flexible with your structure. However, running through the above elements will help define specific meetings that you need to have and make each of those meetings more effective.

And finally, before you announce a meeting, be very clear on one thing: What do I want my team members to do after this meeting?

You will be amazed at the clarity that answering that one question will bring.

Is Your Team Model Broken?

"Have you set high standards in the past to make it clear what
performance you demand?"

Tom Peters

I have encountered too many managers whose team isn't
operating anywhere near its peak potential. The problem
is, many of them don't even know that their team is
underperforming. They feel like they are achieving a lot but
when I help them to really open their eyes, they realise they
are not achieving nearly as much as they should be or growing
as fast as they could be.

There are three indicators that I always look out for when
determining if a manager has a broken team. As a manager,
you should always be on the lookout for them because the
first step towards a productive team is becoming aware that
your team is broken. Real progress comes from awareness, so
watch out for these three warning signs:

1. Constant firefighting in your business

This one you might find difficult to identify at first. You can
often feel like you are doing a good job as a manager when
you're holding the team together, catching mistakes and fixing
them swiftly. You can feel like a superman/superwoman when
you're out there, fixing the problems in your business. The
question is, are you *constantly* doing this? Are the problems in
your business something that crops up on a day-to-day basis?

If so, then your team isn't doing what they're meant to be. Don't get me wrong – everyone makes mistakes and problems do happen in even the best businesses. There will always be fires to fight. But the problems that you're solving should be exceptions, not the rule.

If solving problems in your business is a part of your regular day, then you need to reconsider how your team is structured and how they are working.

2. Micromanagement becoming necessary

Do you find that if you're not there, deadlines seem to slip? Do you constantly have to create timelines and task lists for your team members for them to get things done?

Then you're micromanaging and that's not going to help your business move forward. If you feel that you can't trust your team to deliver what they're meant to deliver on time, most of the time, then there's an issue with how your team is being managed.

3. Every discussion becomes aggressive or sensitive quickly

You need to be able to communicate with your team members. You need to be able to realign their path and assign tasks without fuss and drama. If sensitivity quickly becomes a big issue whenever you try and talk to your team, your competition is going to take over quickly.

The key here is whether there's trust and understanding; if they do not understand you and you do not understand them, then someone will usually take offence and discussions become difficult. You start to ask yourself: What's the point in even bringing it up? I might as well just do it myself. As soon as you think those words, then you know you have an issue with communication in your team and you may need to reconsider your management style.

If you're experiencing any of these signs, then your team simply isn't working the way it should be. The result is that you're carrying the team and, realistically, you were probably better off doing things by yourself. You're not getting the leverage from your team that you should be getting if you want to see your company grow and expand.

In the end, your team is your reflection. So, if you do figure out that your team appears to be broken, consider that your team is as good as your leadership/management style. Take ownership of this situation and sit down to think it through. Ask yourself how YOU can change to make your team better.

Building a Winning Team

"You don't build a business. You build people and
then people build the business."

Zig Ziglar

No successful big business owner is an island. You can keep a business running by yourself, but if you are ready to achieve growth, if you are ready to expand, then you need a team surrounding you.

But you cannot simply hire anyone to work with you. Your team must be right specifically for your business. They need to fit into your culture, they need to have the skills the company needs and that no one else on the team has.

The recruitment process we devise helps towards this end. However, beyond learning how to hire the right people, here are five other important elements that distinguish winning teams from failing ones.

1. Strong Leadership

They say a chain is only as strong as its weakest link. While it is true that the lower boundary is set by the weakest member, the upper boundary is set by the leader – and that may not be the strongest member.

It is important to hire team members who are better than you in the areas that they are hired for. This means that as a team you can achieve more. However, if you are unable to lead them and direct the flow of that teamwork towards the goals of the business, their strengths will be either unused or wasted.

Being a leader means being visible to your team, having the ability to motivate your team, and being able to express to your team WHY they are doing what they do to stimulate that motivation.

2. A Common Goal

And what is leadership without a goal to strive for? No matter what your skills are as a leader, if you do not know what path you are leading them down, you are not taking them down the most successful route.

Everyone on your team should know what they are aiming for individually, and how their goals contribute to the larger goal of the business. If you were to ask each of your team members what was the goal for the next quarter, or the next year, would they answer similarly? Would their answer match your answer?

If they have a 'sense' of it, that is not enough; in an organisation, everyone should have absolute clarity on what the common goal is.

3. Non-Negotiables

This isn't the guidelines or the culture or the values system; I have consciously used the term 'rules of the game' because we really are playing a professional game here.

Your business is not a gathering of family members where it is a bit fuzzy and emotional. Even if you are a family-owned business, when it comes to the times you are operating the business, you are not acting as family members at that time. We are professionals and we are playing roles in this business. Good feelings augment that in the best way, but at the core this is a professional sport.

What you are aiming for here is a 'loose-tight culture'. You should set some clear boundaries for what is acceptable, and then within those boundaries the culture should be loose and innovative. The best teams have the room to be creative, to take risks and to try new things, while keeping within limits of what is non-negotiable to ensure that innovation is directed towards results and not simply wasted energy.

Setting these rules is not the entirety of this element though. The rules of sports are not just written down; if a player goes outside a boundary, there is a clearly defined consequence. What those consequences are for your business you must decide for yourself. They will be different depending on the kind of boundaries you have set, the kind of team you have and the effect on the business.

But what is important is does your team know what the consequences are for not playing within the rules of your game? Talk is easy, but can you implement?

4. Action Plan

With strong leadership, a common goal and a set of boundaries for success set up, you now need to make sure you have a clear action plan in place. Knowing where you are headed is quite different from knowing how you are going to get there.

In the end, you are not managing a team, you are managing their activities. This means you need to lay out a plan for the business and then, importantly, share that plan with your team. Sit down with them and run over how that cascades down to each of them. Where are their responsibilities? What are they accountable for? What do they have ownership of?

Remember that business is a professional game and this is a team sport. There are few team sports where the players go out there and wing it; each has their position on the field and they have a role in the play that the coach and captain have agreed upon to try and win. Sometimes roles need to adjust as a curve ball changes where the critical action is, but then they return to their core responsibilities when the game readjusts.

There needs to be a moment – multiple moments – throughout the year where you pause and reflect on your plan. Business owners need to do this at least once a quarter and include their team members to ensure they are aligned with the plan, working together and clear about the common goal.

5. Effective Management

The final element is understanding that management is what pushes a team forward. Leadership pulls a team *together*, but it is through management that you accelerate them.

The distinction between management and leadership is an important one that many business owners miss. Many business owners are great leaders and need to work on their management skills and vice versa, so it is an important element to become familiar with if you want to run a winning team.

One is not better than the other, but they are distinct with their own functions and activities. In a nutshell, management is about making sure that the preparations are in place, that the systems are operating properly and that the proper leverage is being obtained to drive the team and the business forward.

Where your leadership is in explaining to your team WHY they are doing what they do, your management comes in when you are explaining to them HOW they are achieving the goals of the company.

There are, of course, hundreds of elements that affect how and why a team fails or succeeds. However, by keeping a focus on these five elements, you will build a very strong foundation for creating the kind of team that scores goals and wins results for your business.

Work Horses and Problem Children

"The biggest mistake you'll ever make is letting people
stay in your life for longer than they deserve."

Unknown

"Publicly embarrass him into action!"

My client looked at me with a mixture of astonishment and disbelief. We were discussing one of his most capable team members who he felt was not performing at his peak.

Her natural inclination, like many other business owners, was to think of what they could do to motivate the person and jump to start thinking of increasing their pay – so this was not what she was expecting me to say.

I shared with her a framework which helps me make fast decisions on what is more likely to work with different people. The framework simply maps people's level of competence with their ability and willingness to work hard.

On the Y Axis is the competence of the person: their intelligence, experience and general capability of performing the role. On the X Axis is their ability and willingness to work hard, put in long hours and run the laps required. Stop here and plot your team on the grid below before you continue reading.

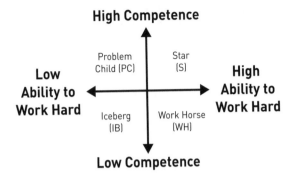

The Iceberg (IB)

Is there a person in your team who you believe is not demonstrating any competence and is also not someone who has shown the willingness to work hard? Often the reason this person is still in your team is because you believe they have potential which has still not shown itself. Like an iceberg, you believe that there is another 90% there which will soon show itself.

There are two options you need to consider for the icebergs in your team: either help them exit the team or change their environment. In either case, they are not a right fit for what they are currently doing or how they are currently doing it and a significant change needs to happen to change them into high performers.

The Star (S)

How many people in your team would you categorise as bringing the best of competence and hard work to the role? These are your stars and the ideal people to hire. Ensure that they are constantly acknowledged and rewarded for being stars. You need to tell them that you really value them, and through guidance, training and direction, keep helping them perform at better and better levels. The extreme top right of the grid is where the superstars are – this is the space which you are consistently trying to hire in.

If you only had stars and icebergs in your team, life would be a lot easier. Unfortunately, people in teams are usually lacking either in competence or in the willingness to work hard.

The Work Horse (WH)

Who are the people in your team who work very hard, are willing to put in whatever hours it takes, are completely devoted to their work but still consistently make mistakes and never quite 'get it'? These are people with a genuine capability constraint – often for no fault of theirs. You cannot see them as leaders and independent workers because they always need to be told what to do and very often also require their work to be checked for quality. While the term 'work horse' may appear derogatory, it is only to indicate that these people are required parts of every organisation as they are usually extremely reliable.

The key to motivate someone in this category is to give them crystal clear instructions on every task and let them do one thing at a time until they really understand what is required of the role. Unclear instructions and non-systemised work environments bring out the worst in them. They will keep slogging away but still be unable to deliver what is really required for the business. You need to invest in training them to be able to increase their capability and bring out the star in them.

The Problem Child (PC)

In my opinion, the people in this quadrant are the least coachable and the most difficult to motivate. These are the smart people in the organisation – the 'I know' people in the team who at some point in their career decided that hard work was not their thing. The only thing that's really holding back this person from being a star is themselves and that's a hard battle to win from the outside.

The more you try to motivate people in this quadrant, the more reasons you will run into as to why things are the way they are and done the way they are doing it. The best strategy I've seen work for people in this quadrant is embarrassing them into action. You need to shake them up by asking 'Is this the best that you can do?' This gives them the message they do not like because, in their mind, their benchmarks are quite high for themselves. A challenge to their way of being leads either to a breakdown or to a breakthrough.

Each person in your organisation has the potential of being a star and even a superstar. However, the reality is that the majority are likely to be in the other three quadrants and need constant nudges to make them either more capable or work harder.

So, here's another interesting question. Where would you plot yourself on this grid? And who is helping you move to being a superstar?

Wednesday is the New Monday

"If everyone is thinking alike, then someone is not thinking."

George S Patton

Most businesses generally start their new hire on a Monday – it's the start of the week, so let's make a new start. What's wrong with this reasoning?

The first few days of a person's role are supposed to be their induction and settling in period. These are also the most likely to be planned: where you sit down with them to train them, get them to sit down with team members to understand their work and the business systems, complete any required employment paperwork, induct and explain company culture and values to them etc.

The first few days are where there is a ton of information that is really downloaded to the new employee and therefore often the most mentally exhausting. By the time they are in the middle of the week, they are potentially feeling overwhelmed. They are at a stage where they do not have a delineation between where the training period ends and where their performance is expected to kick in. They need time to let all the information that they are observing settle down.

Importantly, you need to also be able to step back into a routine and not spend the entire week handholding the new employee.

Now what if the person had started on a Wednesday, so that by the time this overwhelm hits them (and you), we are already nearer the weekend?

Your new employee has had three days to get a good feel of the business, the culture and the values. You've given your best to make sure they have gone through all the parts that they need to understand their role and begin to contribute to the business.

They go away for the weekend, take a break from the intensity of starting a new role and when they come back on Monday, they are feeling fully energised, very clear with the right induction, the right impressions and looking forward to starting to contribute. They are ready to get into their role fully as they are now in their second week.

Remember, first impressions make a big difference and this is a small change that will make a big difference to your business.

Hiring Mistakes

"Hiring the wrong person is the costliest mistake you can make."

Brian Tracy

One of my clients was once looking to hire another IT engineer to join her team. When we sat down to discuss her final selections, she said, "There's something hilarious that happened in one of the interviews. You know we always ask people why they left their previous role. Here's how one of the candidates replied: 'My daily commute is too long. In fact, there are 33 traffic lights between my home and the office.' As I was digesting this, unaided he added, 'And there are only 14 between my home and this office'."

We decided to hire him. For all his quirks, he has proved to be one of her best employees.

For most business owners, recruiting is often a skill they learn through making mistakes. Fortunately, many others have trodden the path before and you do not really need to make your own mistakes, you can simply choose to learn from other people's. Here are a few common mistakes I've seen made repeatedly.

Mistake 1: Vague or Inaccurate Job Specifications

Recruiting with a vague job specification in the belief you will be getting your money's worth by employing someone with a little bit of experience in everything.

Reality: Your job specification is vital to effective recruitment and selection, allowing you to define the kind of person you want and write an accurate job advertisement, assess and compare candidates fairly and make evidence-based selections.

Solution: Clarity is key. Start by listing the weak areas in your business – this will give you an idea of the gaps that need filling. Then list the daily duties and the required skills and experience for each role you have identified. Finally, consider what you offer candidates in return.

Start with the end in mind. If this candidate is already on board, what are this person's deliverables? What is the business objective which needs to be met through this person? For the business objectives to be met, what are the key activities that must be undertaken? What are the Key Performance Indicators?

Mistake 2: Off Target Marketing

Keen to attract the best mix of candidates, you advertise your vacancy everywhere.

Reality: Quantity doesn't mean quality. Advertising without direction, on familiar jobs boards and newspaper columns, encourages passive jobseekers to apply on a whim, often creating more work for you while reducing your chances of finding your ideal candidate. Remember also that recruitment is a two-way street. Your marketing needs to convince quality candidates they should want to work for you.

Solution: Advertise where your target talent will be. In her book *Turn Your Passion To Profit*, Corrina Gordon Barnes advises on creating a 'missing person profile'. Complete the details with visuals and must-haves. Then, tailor your message specifically to that person, reaching out whether they are on social media, industry forums and job boards or local events.

Mistake 3: Omitting Background Checks

Your candidate ticks all your person specification boxes. They have shown their expertise at interview. So why verify their qualifications and eligibility?

Reality: Statistics show that one in three adults lie on their CV. They might sound like an Excel whiz on paper and even in the interview, but if you just take their word for it you might be in for a time-consuming and expensive shock. Equally, checks and references can often reveal crucial need-to-know information. Think you can spot a fake? Don't risk it.

Solution: Verify candidate competencies within the interview process (ideally a combination of psychometric, numeric and technical hands-on exercises). This is both an unbiased way to compare candidates and a decision-making aid, reducing the risk of relying on a CV and interview alone. Run background and safety checks as well as references early, not as an afterthought.

Mistake 4: Looking for the Perfect Candidate Rather than the Perfect 'Fit'

You're so wrapped up in your job specification you forget to factor in personality or vice versa.

Reality: Your company culture and brand values should influence your hiring decisions. According to *Great Place to Work*, one in five employees is disengaged, and if they were fully engaged productivity could double. By choosing a new employee who is truly interested in and passionate about your company's goals and services, you will be hiring your company's next best advocate. Sometimes that might mean hiring someone who has less experience but more energy.

Solution: Hire for skill and culture by employing candidates that match the basic qualifications remembering to screen for a cultural fit.

Mistake 5: Rushing the Hiring Process

You are expanding and you need a position filled, yesterday! So you aim to hire as fast as possible, holding just one round of interviews.

Reality: Picking the best candidate from a bad bunch might seem like your only option if you are keen to fill a post, but really it shouldn't ever be an option. An effective interview process gives you and the candidate ample opportunity to assess each other. Don't skimp on it – you should have at least three stages of interviews: group, task/assessment based and a one-on-one interview.

Solution: If your recruitment campaign has proved fruitless, dedicate an hour a week to regular group interviews and keep going until you find that right fit. Always remember: Hire Slow and Fire Fast.

Mistake 6: No On-Boarding Strategy

You have your ideal candidate, they have started, so now the recruitment process is over.

Reality: Apparently 80% of company leaders offer a substandard induction, leading to one in five new employees leaving a business within the first six months. With the average cost for new employee replacement reaching £30,611 this is an expense you cannot afford. Recruiting doesn't end with the offer being made and accepted, it is vital to plan your new starter's initial journey.

Solution: Develop a detailed on-boarding and induction strategy. Plan a comprehensive induction programme and consider what kit – including technology and company information – your new team member will need. You might even want to consider providing a mentor. Define your employee's KPIs from the outset giving them a sense of direction and purpose right from the day they start.

Mistake 7: Delaying Your Recruitment Plans

You have put off your recruitment plans while you juggle the various roles you really need to fill – and time's really flown!

Reality: Business owners commonly delay implementing their recruitment plans by more than a year. If you consider the amount of time and money you have spent managing tasks you are not the right person for, at the detriment of your real role, has it been worth it?

Solution: Sometimes it is more advantageous to employ a temporary or part-time person to oversee administrative duties. Extra staff doesn't always equal extra cost in the long run. Estimate how much income a new person could help generate – directly or indirectly. Could the new hire release the most important person in the business to focus on expansion, serving more clients or providing a better quality of service? Many businesses realise too late that a well-planned workforce can increase their profitability and growth potential.

Recruitment is not an exact science. You can, however, significantly improve the probability of hiring the right person by making sure that you are learning – best practices and mistakes to avoid – and taking decisive action.

Pay Less to Your Next Employee

"Hire character; Train skill."

Howard Schultz

One of the businesses I was working with was hiring for a senior management position and because of the nature of their business, they did not really have a benchmark salary to offer. We created a job description and requirement document together and advertised the role. Except, to test and measure, we kept everything else the same and advertised the exact same role at two different salary levels: £48,000 p.a. and £100,000 p.a.

Guess what happened? For the role advertised at £48,000 p.a., we received 50+ good applications whereas for the role advertised at £100,000 p.a. we received just one application! For the exact same role!

We've repeated this experiment over multiple roles with split testing to perfect the process for ourselves and several of our clients and are always surprised that we get significantly more applications for the role advertised at a lower salary.

Here's my reading of this: most candidates when searching for jobs end up applying for positions that pay a lower salary due to their own confidence in their abilities.

Employers across the world appear to have become proficient in destroying the confidence and self-esteem of their employees and have left the job market rife with candidates whose own estimated self-worth is far lower than they are worth. There are, of course, happy exceptions to the rule, but these are exactly that – exceptions.

Companies are filled with employees who crave for a better life but lack the courage to look out as they are not confident that they are more valuable. Job markets are filled with disillusioned talented people trying to escape from a role that is simply not right for them.

Given the above, there may be a few changes in your recruitment process that could help you access a much larger pool of good people and potentially great employees.

Step 1: Post a job ad with a lower salary as well

First, post your advertisement for a lower salary than you think you would normally pay for this job and post one at the higher salary too. When working with agencies, split test to ensure that you have different agencies working with different salary levels.

Step 2: Interview candidates and compare

Once you have found someone you think is a winner, interview him or her closely and see how he or she stacks up against those who are demanding a higher pay. How do their qualifications compare? How does their experience and ability to talk about their work compare?

You might be surprised to find someone far better in the lower salary group. The question you should be asking yourself is would you be willing to pay this person what you were offering the higher salary band group?

We recommend the four-hour recruitment process to help businesses effectively get in front of more potential employees; you can access this in the Resources section of our website.

Step 3: Increase their pay

The key, however, is that once someone has completed their probationary period in your business and they have proved their worth, you then need to increase their pay! Make sure that they are being paid more than the market would offer so they will never leave. This is a great incentive structure because not only are you incentivising with money, but also simultaneously emphasising your employee's worth to the business.

This kind of encouragement and self-esteem building is invaluable – and will earn you loyal employees every time. We have seen it happen time and again, and it is a simple process to implement in just about any business.

As a business owner, creating employment opportunities is one of the ways you are already giving back to society. Make sure that the people who do work with you come to work every day wanting to contribute and getting the acknowledgement and validation they deserve.

Why You Should Not Manage Your Team

> "Don't speak unless you can improve the silence."

Spanish proverb

It's 'So Hard' To Manage Your Team

I come across this very often when I am working with business owners that it is so hard to manage a team. It is so hard to get the jobs done at the right level and eventually what they do is they say, "I will do it myself because I can do it faster, I can do it better and I know exactly what kind of output I am after."

You Don't Manage People

There is an important distinction that every business owner needs to make. You as a business owner – as a manager and a leader – do not manage people, you manage their activities. For you to manage the activities efficiently and effectively there are two things that you need.

The Two Things You Need To Manage People Efficiently And Effectively

First you need clarity: what are the activities that you want your team members to work on? How will you measure that those activities are being done? That is the first thing for effective team management: clarity of activities and then measurements.

The second thing you need to manage a team effectively is communication or more specifically – the rhythm of communication. What kind of rhythm do you have in your business whether it is on a daily, weekly or monthly basis? Ideally it is daily or weekly as monthly is kind of quite late in the whole process.

Just to also clarify: having a quick conversation, having a quick chat, is not rhythm of communication. This is a system that you need to set in your business, which will help you effectively manage the activities of your team and get the results that you are after.

The Biggest Productivity Lie

> "Don't confuse activity with productivity. Many
> people are just busy being busy."
>
> **Robin Sharma**

I was reviewing a job advertisement one of my clients had placed and noticed that one of the most important requirements he had mentioned for the role was 'Ability to multitask'.

Now this isn't uncommon for businesses; there are fewer people and a lot of different things to do so most roles require an ability to multitask. Don't they?

I believe that multitasking is a lie. As Steve Uzzell says, it is just an opportunity to screw up more than one thing at a given time.

Not Meant For Human Beings

In fact, multitasking was not even a word meant for human beings. Around 1960, in the early days of the computer when a 10 MHz speed was considered mind boggling, the term 'multitasking' first began to be used, and it meant a computer performing multiple tasks *alternately*.

When the context changed and multitasking started being used for human beings, it began to be understood as multiple tasks being done *simultaneously*.

Human Brains CAN Do Multiple Things At The Same Time

The truth is that our brains can do multiple things at a given time: we can walk and chew gum at the same time, we can drive while listening to music. The crucial difference is that most of the activities being 'multitasked' are in the zone of our Unconscious Competence. Our brains are not designed to focus on two things at a given time. It must switch back and forth to pay attention to one thing at a time.

But How Does This Matter?

What is the implication of this for our effectiveness in our day-to-day business life? It lays out an approach that is likely to be a lot more effective than what people generally use.

Imagine a very distracted way of working: you start task A and you get about a quarter of the way through. Suddenly somebody knocks on your door and says, "Boss, can I have a minute with you?" Now your mind must switch, it must reorient for that distraction. You spend some time on that distraction and then your brain has to switch again and reorient for task A and perhaps after another hour or so you will complete the task. What should have taken you 30 minutes has taken you more than an hour.

If when you come into your office you decide that task A is really the most important thing you can get done today, you close your door and focus completely on the task for 30 minutes before even checking your emails. Thirty minutes later you finish task A and can get back to speaking to your team or responding to emails. This is the focused approach – no interruptions, no distractions. You just focus on one thing and you get it done.

According to some research, the additional time spent on a task when using an unfocused approach is more than 25% for simple tasks and often even beyond 100% for more complex tasks.

So, Ask Yourself, Should You Multitask? And Should You Expect Your Team to Multitask?

If you find yourself thinking at the end of every day and every week: Where did the time go? ask yourself: Did I actually manage to achieve the key things that I had to achieve today? If the answer is no, perhaps multitasking is killing your productivity and making you less effective even if you spent the entire day and week feeling extremely efficient.

The easiest way of disabusing yourself from the myth of multitasking efficiency is to make sure that you pick one key thing to achieve every day and focus completely on it when you start your work and until you have completed it. Do nothing else if this task is not completed.

What's the one thing you could do today that would give you a sense of accomplishment and help your business move forward?

Are You a 'Got a Minute' Boss?

"Anyone who inhabits himself cannot believe in objective thinking."

Hugh Prather

Imagine you work for Sir Richard Branson as one of his senior sales managers. You need to discuss the sales forecast for the following year. And it's quite important because there are a few things which you are not clear about which you need his input and approval on before you go out and announce it to the entire team.

Here's Scenario A. You knock on his door and say, "Got a minute, Richard?" And Richard Branson says, "Yes, of course, tell me." You go in and sit down, you have a chat with him, you tell him what's going on in your mind and some issues that you were thinking about. You also take this opportunity to let him know how other things are going for you – personally and in the organisation. Finally, Richard says, "Listen, leave this with me and I'll come back to you with my thoughts."

Here's another way the whole story could play out. Scenario B is where you call Richard's secretary and she gives you a time in his diary: exactly 30 minutes, two days from today. You email him your figures and your questions to go over before the meeting in a few crisp bullet points. You spend the next couple of days polishing what you are going to discuss with him making sure you have thought of all possible scenarios that may come up. And then you get into this meeting.

Which of the above scenarios is likely to result in a better and more productive meeting? Which one do you currently have playing out every day in your business?

Are you an 'Open Door', 'Got a Minute' boss? Or does your team come to you with good preparation, with preplanning, with a proper meeting set in your diary, where you are asking good questions because you're already prepared for the conversation? Do your meetings end with "I'll think about it, leave it with me," or with your team going back with a clear sense of direction and execution?

Your time and attention is one of the most valuable assets in your business. If you don't treat it with respect and continue to fritter it away, why will others around you act any differently? What could you do today to start respecting your own time in the business a little more?

Part VI:
Methodology

"Always assume that your opponent is going to be bigger, stronger
and faster than you so that you learn to rely on technique, timing
and leverage rather than brute strength."

Helio Gracie

My Car is Allergic to Vanilla Ice Cream

"Whatever gets measured gets managed and improved."

Lord Kelvin

The Pontiac Division of General Motors once received the following complaint:

"This is the second time I have written you, and I don't blame you for not answering, because I kind of sounded crazy.

"We have a tradition in our family of ice cream for dessert after dinner each night. But the kind of ice cream varies so, every night, after we've eaten, the whole family votes on which kind of ice cream we should have and I drive down to the store to get it. It's also a fact that I recently purchased a new Pontiac and since then my trips to the store have created a problem.

"You see, every time I buy vanilla ice cream, when I start back from the store my car won't start. If I get any other kind of ice cream, the car starts just fine.

"I want you to know I'm serious about this question, no matter how silly it sounds: 'Why does my car seem allergic to vanilla ice cream?'"

The team at Pontiac was understandably sceptical about the letter, but sent an engineer to check it out anyway. The latter was surprised to be greeted by a successful, obviously well-educated man in a good neighbourhood. He had arranged to meet the man just after dinner so they could go together to the ice cream store. It was vanilla ice cream that night and, sure enough, after they came back to the car, it wouldn't start.

The engineer returned for three more nights. The first night, the man got chocolate. The car started. The second night, he got strawberry. The car started. The third night he ordered vanilla. The car failed to start.

Now the engineer, being a logical man, refused to believe that this man's car was allergic to vanilla ice cream. He arranged, therefore, to continue his visits for as long as it would take to solve the problem. He also started to test and measure. He collected all sorts of data: time of day, type of fuel used, time to drive back and forth, etc.

Soon he got his first clue: the man took *less time* to buy vanilla than any other flavour. Vanilla, being the most popular flavour, was in a separate container at the front of the store for quick pick-up. All the other flavours were kept in the back of the store at a different counter where it took considerably longer to find the flavour and check out.

The power of this data-driven insight was to change the question immediately from "Why is my car allergic to vanilla ice cream?" to a more sensible "Why does the car not re-start when it takes less time?"

Once time became the problem — not the vanilla ice cream – the engineer quickly understood the answer: vapour lock. It was happening every night, but the extra time taken to get the other flavours allowed the engine to cool down sufficiently to start. When the man got vanilla, the engine was still too hot for the vapour lock to dissipate. Here was a genuine technical problem that could be solved.

There are several messages here for the business owner.

First, the customer is always right! Thinking about every issue raised by a customer will go a long way towards improving the quality of your own product/service.

Next, we often confuse correlation with causation. While the customer thought that buying the vanilla ice cream was causing the car to not start, these were merely correlated events and that made the initial complaint sound strange.

Finally, the first step to identifying a solution to any problem is to ask the right question. The more time spent in identifying the right question, the easier it will be to find the solution.

Remember – Questions are often the Answers.

Moving the World

"Give me a lever long enough and a fulcrum on which to place it
and I shall move the world!"

Archimedes

The principles of leverage that Archimedes explained in 220 BC remain as relevant to business today as they are to physics. Leverage in business means increased business efficiency creating more time for the business owner – and more options on where to spend that time.

The typical business owner is usually like the hub of a wheel, with the spokes of the wheel being all the channels of decision making across all aspects of the business that emanate from the business owner.

What's wrong with this picture?

In our desire to control our business we often imprison ourselves. With no written systems to run our business, we also become vulnerable to key individuals within our organisation who, if they leave the company, will significantly set back the potential of the business.

The answer, as the multinational logistics company Fedex has understood, is: Systemise the routine and humanise the exception.

Every business owner should remember that for a true business:

1. Systems run the business.
2. People run the systems.

3. The business owner leads the people towards achieving business goals.

Systemise your business and you will leverage your capacity as the owner. If systems don't run your business, you are merely another employee in your own company and you will not be able to extract yourself to work on your business instead of in your business.

Getting the right team members on board is leverage, and when you have a recruitment and an induction system for your new team members, you can use it again and again to hire the right people for your team.

Testing, measuring and systemising your marketing campaigns is leverage: you spend time, effort and investment right now to understand what works for your business and you can use this marketing strategy for quite a while.

Creating documentation and a system module for your operations or production line is leverage: you move knowledge from your mind to a place where others in your team can access it.

Borrowing money from the bank is also leverage: you don't wait for your own cash flow to catch up with your growth, you use financial leverage to get to your end result faster.

Every tradesman uses tools to perform his craft. One of the most important tools in the business owner's tool box is the lever. Choose to use it. You may just move the world!

The Outsourcing Pyramid

"If you deprive yourself of outsourcing and your competitors do not, you're putting yourself out of business."

Lee Kuan Yew

Outsourcing in any sense – working with outsourced team members or with outsourcing providers – is usually motivated by the need to scale up the business. If you are planning on growing your business through outsourcing, then it is essential that you learn how to set up systems correctly to maximise the leverage in your business.

If your outsourced providers are not performing the way you would like them to, it may point to the need to improve your own systems.

Optimising your systems is about ensuring that you construct them with a good knowledge of the three basic layers of systems. Using these, you can then create systems that will help your outsourced partners know what you need clearly, and help you drive your business forward.

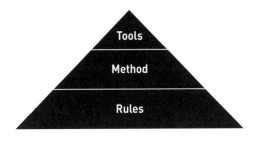

Base Layer: Rules and Policies

Systems are like pyramids, and the bottom of that pyramid is the Rules and Policies layer. The first thing you need to be clear about is the direction in which your company is headed, and what you are committed to. What are your values? Your values will drive the company's values. Have you spelled out any regulations in your business? Have you written down the culture that you have or hope to build in your business?

These values, rules and policies in your business are essential for outsourcing work. Everyone working for your business needs to first and foremost understand the values you want to uphold in your business, and the rules they need to adhere to. This is true not just for the people working alongside you, your employees, but even more so for those who are outsourced and are a step removed from the culture that you create in an office environment.

Have you documented your purpose and goals and the expectations of your clients to define how people are expected to work?

This layer of systems also includes legal details, contracts, policies, and any conditions or constraints that are placed on your employees – including confidentiality and non-compete clauses.

Start off your communication with your outsourced provider by making every expectation explicit and you are setting them up to win – for themselves and for your business.

Middle Layer: Method

Once the Rules and Policies have been defined, the next layer details out the process and procedures – the method of doing – required in the business.

Processes are logically related tasks that translate your rules and policies into actions. So, in any system the tasks that get you from input to output are the process. Setting this up is best done using a process chart.

Procedures are the detailed instructions that tell you step by step how to achieve a process. So while a process states 'this needs to be done', the procedure tells you 'this is how you do it'.

Procedures act as quality control by ensuring it is clear how you get the required output.

For example, let's say you have an outsourced virtual assistant who handles many of the accounts tasks in your business. Here's how the process and procedure may be:

Process Step: Back Up Company Account File

Procedure:

1. Take the company file from the folder that has the label Company Accounts.

2. Copy the file that has today's date written in the date field.

3. Save this into the Cloud storage and copy it on to the physical hard drive and label it with [date] Company Accounts.

Top Layer: Tools

The very top of the system pyramid are the tools that you use to distribute this system to your employees or outsourced workers. Many people when building systems start (and end) here – they start with figuring out how they will communicate with their workers who are sitting outside their office. If they start with the first two layers and work up to here, it often becomes a lot clearer and easier to do.

Your tools can be items such as checklists, forms, templates, guides etc. It is the documentation or the physical items that you use to communicate your processes and procedures to the relevant people.

Let's demonstrate with a simple example from McDonald's. During the sales process, a step in their process is that the person at the counter needs to upsell. The procedure is to ask, "Would you like fries with that?" and do so with a smile. The tool will be the handbook in which this procedure has been written down for the employee to read and learn.

Common tools that most businesses have are how-to manuals and videos. Generally, almost every business should have a manual for each position in their business. The manual spells out the processes and procedures that person needs to complete their function effectively in your business. It should form an integral part of your induction process, but developing these sorts of manuals for your outsourced positions as well is incredibly useful for ensuring that they are performing the work in the way you want them to.

Remember, however, that your outsourced provider, no matter how detailed your manual, will put their own style into achieving the final product. That is why it is essential to build these from a foundation of rules and policies and a description of the overarching process. The procedures in the manual should be the essential parts for the systemised part of the job, but if you've set the other layers right, then the person should be able to handle any exceptions from those systemised parts in a manner which is in line with your business goals and culture – even if they do not have you looking over their shoulder!

If you build your systems for your outsourced workers with these three layers in mind, you can start really leveraging the power of outsourcing without diluting your company's culture or requiring exceptional levels of quality control.

Mastering the production of systems can then mean you can create smooth automation, which allows you to let large parts of your business run effectively without your constant intervention.

Boring is Interesting

"Repetition is a form of change."

Peter Schmidt

In 140 BC, some savvy Roman politicians devised a plan to win the votes of their citizens and make sure they did not revolt. They figured that as long as people had (a) enough to eat and (b) enough distractions, they would not contest those rising to power. They coined the phrase 'Bread and Circuses'. They were of course referring to wheat rations and the gladiator fights among other things.

Over 2,000 years later, the nature of the 'Bread' and the nature of the 'Circuses' have changed. What has not changed is their importance in determining how motivated any group of people is to challenge the status quo. A well-fed stomach and a good game of footy are often enough to make most people happy.

So why are we talking bread and circuses in a business book? Because these two reasons often define what drives the entrepreneur. 'Bread' could be simply bottom line profit, but is often higher up in Maslow's hierarchy of needs and is related to Belonging or even Esteem. 'Circuses' relate to the everyday excitements of going out there and solving problems: finding customers, converting sales, delivering a first-class job or chasing the next shiny object.

While 'Bread' is often the underlying theme of the business owner's role, their long-term goal and dream, the daily struggle, is often led by the 'Circuses'. What business owners sometimes forget as they ride their daily merry-go-rounds is that often what their business does best has already been identified and just needs to be painstakingly and 'boringly' repeated. The entrepreneur in them, used to the roller coaster of running a business, tends to keep seeking and attracting the next thrill, often at the expense of core strategies that are guaranteed to work and improve their business. Not that they've not tried these, in fact quite the opposite – they have tried them quite successfully. For that very reason, they don't want to do it again, they're bored. They want to do something different.

Here's the definition of boring that I like: *The act or process of making or enlarging a hole!*

When digging for oil, the first drill that is sent down is often a very thin one. At this point, we're just trying to confirm there is oil down there and enough if it. Some entrepreneurs think of themselves as responsible for these oil finds. So, what do they do once the oil is found? They leave that hole and go and start looking elsewhere. Pop Quiz: How many of the five largest companies in the world (by revenue) explore oil? Four of them. How many of these four start looking elsewhere when they hit a reserve and don't do the boring process of enlarging the hole they just made to extract, refine and then sell the oil?

Now answer this question: What's the boring bit of your business that you have been avoiding which you know will have a massive positive impact on your bottom line?

Here's the lesson: embrace the boring parts of your business and you will be shocked at how much value you will release into your business – not least because you stop yourself chasing the shiny objects. Stop the Circus.

The Winning Scoreboard

"Success is a lousy teacher. It seduces smart people
into thinking they can't lose."

Bill Gates

One of my friends is an avid cricket fan and passionately rejects the Indian Premier League, the cricket league played out of India which focuses on a shorter form of the game. Once in conversation while the league was on, he mentioned that he had been studiously avoiding watching any matches maintaining that the series was trivial from the perspective of cricket. Interestingly, he checked the scoreboard every day and knew which teams were doing well and how Eoin Morgan was faring.

I will not go into the long debate we had over how India had redefined cricket, but more interestingly from a business perspective, I wanted to marvel again at how much we take the scoreboard for granted in all sports and ignore it in the one sport where a lot of us spend most of our time – the sport of business!

Imagine two teams playing for the whole day with no scoreboard to keep track of who is winning. At the end of the day, they congratulate each other for a good game played and go home, then come back again the next day to repeat the show. After a week of doing this, how keen do you think the captain is going to be to keep motivating his team? How excited is the team going to be to get out of bed every day and get to the field? Can you see the spectator stands in the second week? Are they bursting with people cheering the teams on?

As absurd as it may sound, this is how most business owners play their sport. And then they wonder why their team is not motivated, why the banks refuse to lend to them and why customers are not flocking to their doorstep. Most will glance at their profit and sales figures at the time of the year when their accountant tells them they are legally obliged to do so. They will also keep an eye on their bank balance to make sure they can pay today's bills and come back for another day of play. Is this enough?

Many of the systems that are really required for a good business scoreboard don't require anything other than simple personal discipline to test and measure, every day, every week and every month. It seems like a major undertaking at the start but like many tasks, when organised, established and routine it takes just a few minutes a day. This scoreboard once built will give an instant perspective on your business's performance for the previous week.

The content will vary from business to business; however, typical content might be as follows for the past week:

Winning Business:

- How many Leads did you receive?
- Where did they come from? (e.g. Referrals, Website, Telemarketing, Local Advertisements)
- How many Sales did you make? What was your Conversion Rate?
- What was the Value of your Sales?
- What was the Average Value per Transaction?

Financials:

- What were your Invoiced Sales?

- What was your Gross Profit?

- What were the Cash Receipts?

- What was the Bank Balance at the close of the week?

- How many Debtor and Creditor Days did you have at close?

Operations:

- How many Direct Labour Hours were available for production or service delivery?

- How many Direct Labour Hours were invoiced this week?

- What is the Measure of Time Expected versus Time Taken on jobs and tasks?

- What is the Percentage Right First Time?

- What was the value of Wastage?

 Most businesses can put a skeleton of a scoreboard together quite quickly and improve it as they go along. You can also access a template from the Resources section of our website.

The important thing to focus on when you have your scoreboard is a regular review to reflect on the wins, challenges and learning for the week. It makes sense to set time aside to do this at a regular time each week and compare the results with pre-set targets which are stretching yet achievable and realistic. Some of these might be Key Performance Indicators looking at activity, whereas some will be outcomes or Key Results Indicators. Some of these measures may be more complex than others but once these are captured, there will often be some obvious massive improvements which could be made to the business to improve the bottom line.

Whether there's a need to focus on more sales activity, sales performance, more marketing effort, better cash collection systems, or operational efficiency, the adage applies: You can't manage what you don't measure. Without a scoreboard, you are not really managing your business.

The Business BRAIN

"My brain is the key that sets me free."

Harry Houdini

More than half the childbirths in the UK require some form of intervention. The problems which occur during labour often require critical decision making: natural birth or caesarean? IV or fluids? Use medicines to speed up the delivery?

Each intervention has a consequence which could have lasting effects for the newborn or mother or both. These decisions do not just require critical thinking under time pressure but are also at moments which are rife with emotions.

In such situations, the decision-making process is aided through the BRAIN framework. This practical tool not only helps deliver healthy babies but can also help you deliver healthy business results.

Let's look at an application of the BRAIN model in a business scenario.

Imagine you are thinking of hiring a person for an important sales position which will potentially help you generate more revenue. There is, however, a large upfront outlay in the form of high salary and perks. Often, when faced with decisions like these, business owners choose to rely on their intuition aided by how confident they are feeling at that time about the future.

Intuition in the business is powerful but can be disastrous if it is the only aid to your decision making. Instead, analyse on a piece of paper the Benefits, Risks and Alternatives of the decision and then bring in Intuition and a final question.

Benefits

What are the benefits of hiring this person for the sales position?

Risks

What are the risks involved?

Alternatives

Are there any alternatives? Is there another way for me to solve the problem I'm looking to solve? What are the other possible solutions?

Intuition

What does my intuition say? Does this hire make sense?

Starting with this question could cloud your objectivity and lead to stickiness in your choice but harnessing it at this stage makes intuition your powerful ally.

Nothing

What if we did nothing? Or waited a while?

Most business owners by nature are driven, hard-working and prefer action to inaction; doing nothing is often not an option. Remember that 'focus' is also about knowing what not to do.

It is good practice to consider your decisions objectively every time and a framework or model helps you do this – even in situations where you are strongly for or against a certain decision already. The BRAIN model can in these cases help build your own Business Brain.

More
Sparks

"Perhaps the worst sin in life is knowing right and not doing it."

Martin Luther King

As a business owner, you probably have access to tons of information. Often, however, people do not appreciate the fact that information is only a very small part of what is required to succeed – only the tip of the iceberg.

An example is the phrase 'Eat Less, Exercise More'. Most people have the core information required to maintain a healthy weight. The crucial question, of course, is that when the 'secret' is so straightforward, why are so many people still overweight?

I believe that most people in life know enough of 'what' to do and 'how' to do it. If they do not, the information is usually accessible. But knowing is not their main issue. Bridging the gap between knowing and actual results is where business coaching comes in.

There are four key reasons people choose coaching. 'What' to do – the ideas, strategies, tactics and information – is only one of them.

When you hire an employee, to ensure that they are successful, you give them measurable results to achieve, monitor their activities and performance rigorously and make sure that you continually hold them accountable to achieve what you have set them to achieve. Who holds the business owner accountable? I find that people are often too hard on others and too soft on themselves whereas it should, in fact, be the exact opposite. A key role of a coach is to ensure accountability to business objectives set alongside the business owner.

The third key benefit of a coach is the reason why almost every professional sportsperson has one: objectivity. When you are out there on the field, who's watching your shots?

Who's giving you genuine and constructive feedback on how to improve your game? The coach is often the objective outsider to your industry who can observe and correct your game – while you play.

And finally, being part of a coaching community ensures that you treasure and guard your environment; you surround yourself with business owners who are all working towards greatness and ensuring they maintain a positive mindset. What has worked for other business owners who have been through the same stages of growth that you are going through right now? What are the mistakes others made when they were doing what you are doing in your business right now? Who else, besides you and your coach, is watching your back?

If you believe that you are ready to take on the next level of growth for your business, and are open to being helped to achieve even more in your business journey, reach out to me – through filling out the simple business alignment questionnaire (BAQ) on our website – www.londoncoachinggroup.com/baq.

I would love to hear from you!

Remember the magic catalyst for transformation is always Action.

Resources

 All materials and resources referred to in this book can be accessed through www.londoncoachinggroup. com/sparks. Please use the code $PARK$ to access the material.

To continue to receive more sparks, please like our Facebook page: https://www.facebook.com/BusinessCoachingLondon

About the Author

Shweta Jhajharia is a serial entrepreneur, an international business speaker and a leading global business coach. Founder of the London Coaching Group, an ActionCOACH company, she has personally worked with hundreds of businesses.

Shweta is a multi-award winner (her awards include two prestigious International Stevie awards, a Millionaire Coach Award and the British Franchise Association's Judges Award) and has been featured by more than 50 media outlets including BBC, *FT Adviser*, *City AM*, *Training Journal*, *Evening Standard* and *Management Today*.

Best known for her no-nonsense, growth-focused approach, Shweta has helped business owners across sectors consistently achieve measurable double-digit growth alongside productive teams and robust systems.

Before turning to entrepreneurship, Shweta was a Global Marketing Manager at Unilever. She also has an MBA from the Indian Institute of Management. She lives in London with her husband Amol and son Vedant. She enjoys mountain climbing (her last climb being Kilimanjaro), squash, and travelling.

Find out more about Shweta and her work at www.londoncoachinggroup.com